LIFE'S BIG QUESTIONS

RULES and DIRECTIONS

VAUGHAN ROBERTS

LIFE'S BIG QUESTIONS

Six major themes
traced through the Bible

ivp

Inter-Varsity Press

INTER-VARSITY PRESS
38 De Montfort Street, Leicester LE1 7GP, England
Email: ivp@uccf.org.uk
Website: www.ivpbooks.com

First published 2004
Reprinted 2004, 2005

British Library Cataloguing in Publication Data
A catalogue record for this book is available from the British Library.

ISBN 1–84474–021–8

Set in Dante 10.5/13pt
Typeset in Great Britain by CRB Associates, Reepham, Norfolk
Printed and bound in Great Britain by Creative Print & Design
(Wales), Ebbw Vale

*Inter-Varsity Press is the publishing division of the Universities and
Colleges Christian Fellowship (formerly the Inter-Varsity Fellowship), a
student movement linking Christian Unions in universities and colleges
throughout Great Britain, and a member movement of the
International Fellowship of Evangelical Students. For more information
about local and national activities write to UCCF, 38 De Montfort Street,
Leicester LE1 7GP, email us at email@uccf.org.uk, or visit the UCCF
website at www.uccf.org.uk.*

Contents

To Siân and Clare

Acknowledgments

I am very grateful to James Dudley-Smith for commenting on the manuscript and to Glenn B. Nesbitt for comments, typing and much else besides.

Introduction

'You can make the Bible say whatever you want'

An article in a university's Student Union newspaper recently attacked Christian Union members for their approach to the Bible:

> These people plunder the pages in search of sound bites: phrases to fit specific dilemmas, sentences to condemn the ungodly ... The funniest thing, though, is that I am sure I can find a quotation saying the exact opposite to anyone who bashes me with biblical curses. This book is not a whole. It was not all written 2,000 years ago by a biblical Jackie Collins. There are different texts by different authors, in very different contexts: to treat them as a whole is a downright travesty.[1]

It is a familiar charge: 'You can make the Bible say whatever you want,' we are told. Of course, that is right; you can. In the arguments over whether Jesus is the only way to God, or the morality of homosexual sex, both sides quote Scripture. Is that because there is contradictory teaching in the Bible, so that it supports both positions in different places? Or is it because one of the groups, at least, is misinterpreting it?

The answer depends on the nature of the Bible. The student writer has focused on the key issue: is it a single book, a whole, a unity or not? If not, we cannot expect it to speak with one voice. There will be different strands of teaching that often contradict each other; so we will be free to pick and choose whichever parts suit us. But if the Bible is a whole, that approach will not be open to us. Instead, we will need to work hard to see how the different parts fit together.

The Bible is one book

The Bible certainly contains a diverse collection of writings: sixty-six books written by about forty different human authors over a considerable period of time. But it still holds together as a unity. Fundamentally, it is just one book written by one author with one main subject. The author is God. The apostle Paul wrote: 'All Scripture is God-breathed' (2 Timothy 3:16). What the human authors wrote still bears the marks of their different personalities, situations and writing styles, but it is not simply their message; it is God's Word. He ensured by his Spirit that they wrote exactly what he wanted them to write. As a result, they combine to present a united message that focuses on one main subject: Jesus Christ and the salvation God achieves through him. Jesus said, speaking of the Old Testament: 'These are the Scriptures that testify about me' (John 5:39). The Old Testament points forward to him as the coming Saviour. The New Testament proclaims him to be that Saviour and calls on all people to believe and obey him.

Promise ⟶ Fulfilment

OT　　　　　　　　　　　　　　　　　　　　NT

Figure 1. God's plan

The unity of the Bible should have significant implications for the way in which we read it. We should be aware not just of the immediate context of a text (the chapter or book in which it is found), but of the overall context (how it fits in the Bible as a whole). We need to have a sense of the framework of the Bible to help us to work out how an individual text fits within it. That is the aim of my previous book, *God's Big Picture*. It seeks to give a chronological overview of the Bible's story-line, starting at Genesis and ending in Revelation. That should equip readers to navigate their way around the Scriptures.

If *God's Big Picture* provides a map of the Bible, *Life's Big Questions* aims to help readers know how to use it. I will take six different themes and see how each unfolds through Scripture. I have deliberately chosen a wide range of subjects: our identity as humans, money and possessions, sex and marriage, mission and the Holy Spirit. I hope that this will give the reader confidence to begin to apply the same methodology to other themes.

It will help if you have read *God's Big Picture* first, but that is not essential. The first chapter of this book looks at the theme of God's king in the Bible. It will cover ground familiar to readers of the previous book, showing how the Bible focuses on Christ. This should provide a bridge between the two books, repeating the framework of *God's Big Picture*, which will also undergird the following chapters.

1 | The once and future King
Who rules the world?

In *God's Big Picture* I followed Graeme Goldsworthy's lead in seeing the kingdom of God as the unifying theme in Scripture.[1] Some prefer to focus on the concept of covenant when showing how the whole Bible fits together. These two approaches are not contradictory. Whereas the dominant theme in the Old Testament is covenant, the kingdom of God is central in the New. The expression is rare in the Old Testament, but it is Jesus' preferred way of referring to his mission, which he understood to be a fulfilment of what had been promised before. It is in the kingdom he is establishing that God's people can finally enjoy all the blessings of the covenant.

Goldsworthy defines the kingdom as 'God's people, in God's place, under God's rule'.[2] *God's Big Picture* traced this theme through the Bible by seeing its development in eight sections, which are the main epochs in God's unfolding plan to restore his kingdom.

In *Life's Big Questions* we will look at six important biblical themes and see how they develop at the different stages of God's revelation. We begin with a subject that is central to the message of the Bible and the kingdom of God: the king.

The Old Testament

1. The pattern of the kingdom – creation before the fall
2. The perished kingdom – the fall
3. The promised kingdom – God's covenant promises
4. The partial kingdom – the promises are partially fulfilled in Israel's history
5. The prophesied kingdom – the prophets point to a final future fulfilment

The New Testament

6. The present kingdom – Jesus is king
7. The proclaimed kingdom – the good news of Jesus is taken to the ends of the earth
8. The perfected kingdom – Jesus returns to introduce the new creation

Figure 2. An overview of the Bible

1. The pattern of the kingdom – God is king of creation

The Bible begins by declaring: 'In the beginning God created the heavens and the earth' (Genesis 1:1).

God made the world and so he has authority over it; he is the king. He has the right to set the rules and to expect obedience. Those rules are always for our good; we suffer if we disobey them. In the Garden of Eden he tells Adam: 'You are free to eat from any tree in the garden; but you must not eat from the tree of the knowledge of good and evil, for when you eat of it you will surely die' (Genesis 2:16–17). As we will see in chapter 2, human beings are given responsibility over the rest of the created order, rulers under God's rule (Genesis 2:26–28). But our authority is not independent of God; it is to be exercised under him.

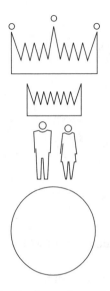

Figure 3. The pattern of the kingdom: rulers under God's rule

2. The perished kingdom – God's rule is rejected

We humans like the thought of being kings in God's world, but we do not want to be kings under him. Genesis 3 describes the rebellion of Adam and Eve. Their disobedient eating from the tree of the knowledge of good and evil symbolizes their rejection of God's rule and their decision to set themselves up as independent rulers. All human beings have followed in their footsteps ever since. The results have been disastrous. Bad rulers have devastating effects: Hitler, Stalin, Idi Amin and Saddam Hussein destroyed their countries, and our rebellious attempt to rule independently of God has had terrible consequences for the whole world. It has led to economic injustice, warfare, ecological crisis and broken relationships. We human beings have fallen as a result of our sin and we have dragged the whole of creation down with us; we live in a fallen world (thus the shading in Figure 4).

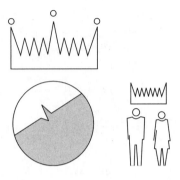

Figure 4. The perished kingdom: fallen rulers in a fallen world

3. The promised kingdom – God will rule through a king

God is determined to re-establish his kingdom and put everything right again. He begins with one man: Abraham. There are three ingredients in the original promise to Abraham, the gospel which is finally fulfilled in Christ:[3]

- *People*: Abraham will have many descendants who will become a great nation (Genesis 12:2)
- *Land*: They will be given a special place to live in (Genesis 12:7)
- *Blessing*: They will be blessed and all nations will be blessed through them (Genesis 12:2–3)

God does not tell Abraham explicitly that he will fulfil his promises through a king, but there are other passages that make this clear:

'... I will put enmity
   between you and the woman,
   and between your offspring and hers;
he will crush your head,
   and you will strike his heel.'
(Genesis 3:15)

God tells the serpent, which represents Satan,[4] that it will be destroyed by a coming saviour. From now on, as we read through the Bible, we are looking for this 'serpent crusher' who will defeat evil and counteract the effects of the fall.

At the end of his life the patriarch Jacob blesses each of his twelve sons. In blessing Judah, he promises that one of his descendants will have an eternal, universal reign:

> The sceptre will not depart from Judah,
>   nor the ruler's staff from between his feet,
> until he comes to whom it belongs
>   and the obedience of the nations is his.
> (Genesis 49:10)

Moses speaks to the people just before they enter the land and tells them that it is God's intention that they should be ruled by a king. He should be an Israelite appointed by God, who submits to God's law. Such a king will lead the nation under God and bring much blessing:

> When you enter the land the LORD your God is giving you and have taken possession of it and settled in it, and you say, 'Let us set a king over us like all the nations around us,' be sure to appoint over you the king the LORD your God chooses. He must be from among your own brothers. Do not place a foreigner over you, one who is not a brother Israelite ... When he takes the throne of his kingdom, he is to write for himself on a scroll a copy of this law ... It is to be with him, and he is to read it all the days of his life so that he may learn to revere the LORD his God and follow carefully all the words of this law and these decrees ... Then he and his descendants will reign a long time over his kingdom in Israel.
> (Deuteronomy 17:14–20)

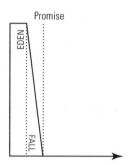

Figure 5. The story so far: promise

4. The partial kingdom – God establishes a monarchy in Israel

Abraham's descendants multiply and become a large tribe. They are persecuted slaves in Egypt, but God does not forget his promises. He redeems them from slavery at the exodus and brings them into a unique relationship with himself. They are given his law and are called to obey it so that they can enjoy his blessing in the Promised Land he has given them. By now, most of God's promises have been fulfilled, at least in part. But there is one crucial missing ingredient: there is no king.

'In those days Israel had no king'

The book of Judges tells the story of Israel's history soon after they have entered the land. A depressing cycle is repeated throughout the book. The Israelites continue to turn away from God and worship idols instead. God responds by judging them, allowing them to be oppressed by their enemies. In their despair they turn to God again and ask for his help. He graciously provides a 'judge' or 'ruler' to rescue them. But soon afterwards, the people return to their wickedness and the cycle begins again.

What is going wrong? A recurring phrase in the book of Judges gives us a clue: 'In those days Israel had no king; everyone did as

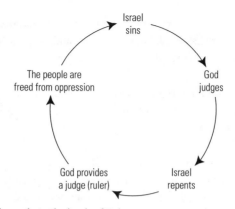

Figure 6. The cycle in the book of Judges

he saw fit' (Judges 17:6; 18:1; 19:1; 21:25). The implication is clear. If only there was a king, of the kind that God had promised before they entered the land, then things would improve.

A false start

The last great judge of Israel is Samuel. In his old age he appoints his sons to succeed him, but they prove to be very different from their father, so the Israelite leaders approach the old man and ask for a change of rule: '... appoint a king to lead us, such as all the other nations have' (1 Samuel 8:5). Both Samuel and God respond with anger.

It is not the request in itself that is wrong; it has always been God's plan that they should be ruled by a king. The fault lies in their motivation. God says to Samuel '... it is not you they have rejected, but they have rejected me as their king' (1 Samuel 8:7). They are not asking for a king under God, but instead of God. They want to be like the other nations, a monarchy rather than a theocracy. As a result, the first king they are given is very different from the kind of monarch God had intended for his people when he spoke to Moses in Deuteronomy 17. Far from helping the people to live under God's rule, Saul disobeys God. He is told to punish the Amalekites for their mistreatment of God's people in the past by totally destroying them and their possessions. But he spares much of the Amalekites' livestock and keeps it for himself and the people. As a result, Samuel tells him:

'Because you have rejected the word of the LORD,
    he has rejected you as king.'
(1 Samuel 15:23)

A king from Bethlehem

Saul continues to reign for a number of years, but as far as the history of salvation is concerned, he is now on the sidelines; God's blessing will not come through him. The focus now shifts to Bethlehem. Samuel is sent by God to visit Jesse because one of his sons has been chosen as king. When he arrives, Samuel sees Eliab, the eldest, and thinks he must be the one because he is so strong and impressive. But God tells him: 'The LORD does not look at the things man looks at. Man looks at the outward appearance, but the LORD looks at the heart' (1 Samuel 16:7). Six other sons of Jesse are then paraded in front of Samuel. No doubt they are all powerful and good-looking; promising king material. But, each time, God makes it clear that they are not the chosen ones, so Samuel asks if Jesse has another son. He replies, 'There is still the youngest, but he is attending the sheep' (1 Samuel 16:11). It has never occurred to him that Samuel might be interested in David, but God says, 'Rise and anoint him; he is the one.' David is anointed and is filled with the Spirit. It is one of the many surprising choices that God makes in the Bible. He chooses 'the lowly things of this world and the despised things – and the things that are not – to nullify the things that are' (1 Corinthians 1:28).

God's presence with David is very evident shortly after his anointing by Samuel. The boy goes to visit his brothers who are fighting on the front line in the war against the Philistines. He is indignant at the way Goliath, the Philistine champion, brings dishonour on God's name by taunting the Israelite army and so he determines to confront him. It looks like a very uneven contest:

an inexperienced boy against a battle-hardened warrior. But David shows no fear and says to Goliath, 'You come against me with sword and spear and javelin, but I come against you in the name of the LORD Almighty, the God of the armies of Israel, whom you have defied. This day the LORD will hand you over to me, and I'll strike you down and cut off your head' (1 Samuel 17:45–46). His faith is vindicated and he wins a great victory. The world seems to be at David's feet. He has been shown to be God's chosen instrument, filled with his Spirit. But his path to the throne is far from straightforward.

Saul is jealous of David and, despite the young man's faithful service, tries to kill him. David is forced to flee and remains a fugitive for many years. As we read of those trials, we are left asking, 'Can he really be the chosen one of God, the anointed, if he is persecuted and rejected in this way?' We can see in his life a foreshadowing of the one who was to come: 'great David's greater son'. He was also anointed by God and received the Spirit at his baptism. He was chased, despised and hated; he was even put to death. But there is no doubt that he was God's choice, God's king.

In the end, David is acknowledged as the king, at first only over his own tribe of Judah, but then over the whole united kingdom of Israel. He conquers Jerusalem, establishing it as his capital city, and brings the ark, symbolizing the presence and rule of God, into the city. David is a very different king from Saul. He seeks to lead the people under God and the result is great blessing. The Israelites have never enjoyed such security before. We even begin to wonder if he might be the 'serpent crusher' of Genesis 3:15 and the great king of the line of Judah who will reign for ever. But it soon becomes clear that he is not.

The son of David

David decides that he should build a permanent resting place for the ark of God. But God speaks to him through the prophet Nathan, telling him that he will not be the one to build the temple; that will be the privilege of a future king from his line:

'When your days are over and you rest with your fathers, I will raise up your offspring to succeed you, who will come from your own body, and I will establish his kingdom. He is the one who will build a house for my Name, and I will establish the throne of his kingdom for ever. I will be is father, and he shall be my son.'

(2 Samuel 7:12–14)

These remarkable promises add to the picture of the saviour king that we have been given. We are now looking for a son of David who will also be a son of God. Surely when he comes, all God's promises will be fulfilled and his kingdom will come.

At first, we wonder whether the great future king might be David's handsome, charismatic son Absalom. He conspires against his father and sets himself up as king. Could he be the one? But his rebellion does not last. As he flees from David's soldiers through a forest, his head is caught by the branches of a tree and he is stuck. Joab, the general, puts a spear through him and that is the end of Absalom (2 Samuel 18).

The focus shifts to Adonijah, another son of David. In David's old age, while the succession is still in doubt, he sets himself up as king. So, could he be the one we have been waiting for? Once again, the answer is no. When David is told of his unilateral bid for the crown, he responds by making Solomon king. Soon after David dies, Solomon puts Adonijah to death and his rule is firmly established.

Solomon: the pinnacle of Israel's history

God appears to Solomon in a dream, saying, 'Ask for whatever you want me to give you' (1 Kings 3:5). Solomon replies:

'O LORD my God, you have made your servant king in place of my father David. But I am only a little child and do not know how to carry out my duties. Your servant is here among the people you have chosen, a great people, too

numerous to count or number. So give your servant a
discerning heart to govern your people ... '
(vv. 7–9)

His humility pleases God, who blesses him greatly. Solomon is the
first king to rule peacefully over the whole land of Israel, without
any attacks from foreign powers. He also builds the temple, which
provides a permanent dwelling place for the ark of God. It is
beginning to look as if God's kingdom has once again been
established on earth. As in the Garden of Eden, his people are
living under his rule in his presence and the result is great blessing.
When he dedicates the temple, Solomon prays, 'Praise be to the
LORD, who has given rest to his people Israel just as he promised.
Not one word has failed of all the good promises he gave through
his servant Moses' (1 Kings 8:56).

But the golden age does not last for long. It soon becomes
clear that Solomon is not the great, eternal king through whom
God's kingdom will fully come. The mood changes in 1 Kings 11.
Solomon marries many foreign wives. His sin is not simply
sexual, it is also spiritual. God had told his people not to
marry Gentiles because they will 'surely turn your hearts after
their gods' (1 Kings 11:2). That is exactly what happens with
Solomon. As he grows old, he begins to turn away from the
LORD and worships foreign gods as well. God is angry with him
and says, 'Since this is your attitude and you have not kept my
covenant and decrees, which I commanded you, I will most
certainly tear the kingdom away from you and give it to one of
your subordinates' (1 Kings 11:11). He is told that the kingdom
will be divided and his son will reign over only a small part
of it.

The divided kingdom
God speaks to Jeroboam, one of Solomon's officials and tells him
that he will rule over ten of the Israelite tribes after Solomon's
death. Solomon's son, Rehoboam, will continue to rule over the

tribe of Judah, so that 'David, my servant, may always have a lamp before me in Jerusalem' (1 Kings 11:36). But Jeroboam's descendants will form an enduring dynasty that will last for many years. God tells him, 'I will humble David's descendants because of this, but not for ever' (v. 39).

It happens just as God had said. Civil war breaks out immediately after Solomon dies and Jeroboam emerges as the leader of the northern kingdom of Israel, with Rehoboam ruling over Judah in the south. 2 Kings and 2 Chronicles tell the story of the kings who succeed them. There are a few godly ones in the midst of a very unimpressive collection, but none like David or Solomon.

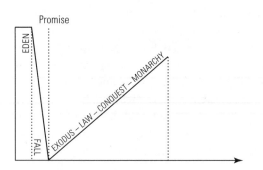

Figure 7. The story so far: the monarchy

5. The prophesied kingdom – a new king will come

Judgment must come
In the centuries after the kingdom was divided in two, the prophets were very active. Their message is dominated by judgment: God must punish the nations for their rejection of his rule. The dynasty of Jeroboam survives in the north, as God had promised, but we know that God's great king will not come through this line. The northern kingdom of Israel is destroyed by

the Assyrians in 722 BC and Jeroboam's dynasty comes to an end. All the focus now shifts to the southern kingdom. Its kings have the right pedigree, being from the tribe of Judah and the line of David. Many of them are ungodly, but some raise expectations, especially Josiah. He leads a religious revival and commits the nation to obeying God's covenant. But this is not the time of fulfilment. The prophets make it clear that God must first judge his people before there can be any sign of hope. Judgment comes on Judah when the Babylonians conquer Jerusalem and capture some of the people in 597 BC. They return to destroy the city and take a much larger group into exile in 586 BC.

A message of hope

In the midst of many dark predictions of doom, some bright messages of hope shine out from the prophetic books. God has not forgotten his promises. They will be fulfilled when God's anointed king, the Christ, comes to reign. This future king will be a son of David, suffering Servant and son of man.

Son of David

Nathan's prophecy in 2 Samuel 7 promised a great king of the line of David, and the prophets tell us that God has not forgotten his promise. Micah foretells that God's king will come from David's town, Bethlehem (Micah 5:2). Isaiah prophesies his birth:

> For to us a child is born,
>   to us a son is given,
>   and the government will be on his shoulders.
> And he will be called
>   Wonderful Counsellor, Mighty God,
>   Everlasting Father, Prince of Peace.
> Of the increase of his government and peace
>   there will be no end.
> He will reign on David's throne
>   and over his kingdom,

establishing and upholding it
  with justice and righteousness
  from that time on and for ever.
(Isaiah 9:6–7)

Those verses make it clear he will be no ordinary king; he is divine. He is not just a son of David, but also the Son of God. Psalm 2 speaks of God establishing his king and then saying to him, 'You are my Son; today I have become your Father' (v. 7). David himself recognizes this future king's superiority over him. He writes:

The LORD says to my Lord:
  'Sit at my right hand
until I make your enemies
  a footstool for your feet.'
(Psalm 110:1)

Who is this Lord, who is not God the Father and yet whom David recognizes as his superior?

The suffering Servant

The early chapters of Isaiah prophesy the coming of a great and mighty king, but the focus in the later chapters is on a rather different figure: a suffering Servant. God's promises to Abraham are only partially fulfilled in the Old Testament because the Israelites keep disobeying God. The world will be restored to the perfection that existed in Eden only once the problem of sin is solved. It is the role of the suffering Servant to achieve that by dying on behalf of his people, so that God will no longer need to judge them. God will then be free to bless them and put everything right again:

He was despised and rejected by men,
  a man of sorrows, and familiar with suffering.

Like one from whom men hide their faces
   he was despised and we esteemed him not.
Surely he took up our infirmities
   and carried our sorrows,
yet we considered him stricken by God,
   smitten by him, and afflicted.
But he was pierced for our transgressions,
   he was crushed for our iniquities;
the punishment that brought us peace was upon him,
   and by his wounds we are healed.'
(Isaiah 53:3–5)

Son of man

Daniel receives visions from God while he is exiled in Babylon. He sees terrifying beasts that represent different kingdoms that will oppress God's people. But Daniel is reassured that these kingdoms will not win in the end; God's kingdom will prevail:

> 'In my vision at night I looked, and there before me was one like a son of man, coming with the clouds of heaven. He approached the Ancient of Days and was led into his presence. He was given authority, glory and sovereign power; all peoples, nations and men of every language worshipped him. His dominion is an everlasting dominion that will not pass away, and his kingdom is one that will never be destroyed.'
> (Daniel 7:13–14)

It is a remarkable promise. God the Father, the Ancient of Days, will give universal and eternal authority to 'one like a son of man'.

After a few decades of exile in Babylon, the people of Judah return to Jerusalem and expectations are high. But no king is appointed and the throne remains vacant. That is when the Old Testament ends. The great days under David and Solomon give hints of what the kingdom of God may look like, but they do not last long. God's kingdom has not come because the king has not come. We are still waiting for the one who will be son of David, son of man and suffering Servant. Surely, when he comes everything will be put right.

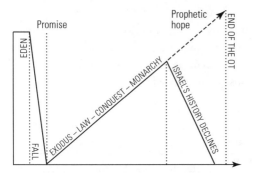

Figure 8. The end of the Old Testament

6. The present kingdom – God's King has come

If David and Solomon were the shadows who gave us an idea of what it means to be ruled by God's king, the reality comes in Christ. He is the son of David, son of man and suffering Servant.

Son of David

Matthew's Gospel begins with these words: 'A record of the genealogy of Jesus Christ the son of David, the son of Abraham' (1:1). He is the one who is promised: Abraham's offspring through whom all nations will be blessed (Genesis 12:2–3) and the great king of David's line (2 Samuel 7:12). He is born in Bethlehem, as Micah said he would be (Matthew 2:1–6). When his public ministry begins, he tells the people, 'The time has come. The kingdom of God is near' (Mark 1:15). It is near because the king has come. He is the one whom David called 'Lord' in Psalm 110:1 (Mark 12:36). The miracles proclaim his power as God's King: at his word demons flee and diseases are healed. At last we are seeing signs of what a renewed creation will look like once God's authority has been re-established through his King. But there are many times when he does not seem very regal, not least as he is arrested and crucified. The cross seems to proclaim his failure, but he does not stay there. The resurrection is God's great declaration to the world that Jesus really is the King. Paul tells the Jews in Antioch, 'What God promised our fathers he has fulfilled for us, their children, by raising up Jesus' (Acts 13:32–33).

Son of Man

'Son of Man' is Jesus' preferred way of referring to himself. When he asks his disciples, 'Who do you say I am?', Peter replies, 'You are the Christ' (Mark 8:29). He has at last realized that Jesus is the divine King, promised in the Old Testament.[5] Then 'Jesus warned them not to tell anyone about him' (Mark 8:30). This 'secrecy motif' is a common theme in Mark's Gospel. It seems Jesus knows that if the news spreads that he is the Christ, he will be under great pressure to conform to the people's expectations. They are hoping for a Christ who will liberate them from the Roman occupying forces and re-establish the independent nation of Israel. But Jesus knows that his mission must be very different, so he wants the fact that he is the Christ to be kept quiet.

Imagine two boxes, one marked 'Christ' and the other 'Son of Man'. The Christ box has already been filled by the misunderstandings of Jesus' contemporaries as to what that title means. If Jesus is to refer to himself as the Christ, he is bound to be misunderstood. He will have to empty the box of the wrong thinking that already fills it before he can put his own right understanding of what it means to be the Messiah into it. By contrast, the 'Son of Man' box is almost empty. It was hardly used as a messianic title in the first century. As a result, Jesus is able to fill the box with his own understanding of his role. That is why he prefers to refer to himself as 'the Son of Man'. So after Peter has said, 'You are the Christ', Jesus immediately shifts the focus away from that title and on to the other: 'He then began to teach them that the Son of Man must suffer many things and be rejected by the elders, chief priests and teachers of the law, and that he must be killed and after three days rise again' (v. 31). He is the great 'son of man' prophesied in Daniel 7.

Jesus also shifts the focus from Christ to Son of Man at his trial before the high priest. He is asked, 'Are you the Christ, the Son of the Blessed One?' He replies, 'I am.' He knows that he is the Christ, but he continues, 'And you will see the Son of Man sitting at the right hand of the Mighty One and coming on the clouds of heaven' (Mark 14:61–62). That is a clear reference to the prophecy of Daniel 7. Jesus is the great universal king whom Daniel saw in his vision, but he must first suffer and die before he enters his glory.

The suffering Servant

Matthew, Luke and John all make it clear that the prophecies of Isaiah 53 that speak of the great suffering Servant have been fulfilled in Christ (Matthew 8:17; Luke 22:37; John 12:38). Mark's Gospel does not explicitly quote from the chapter but the allusions to it are very clear. Jesus says, 'Whoever wants to

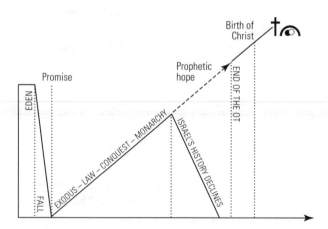

Figure 9. The story so far: the coming of Jesus

become great among you must be your servant, and whoever wants to be first must be slave of all. For even the Son of Man did not come to be served, but to serve, and to give his life as a ransom for many' (10:43–45). The mighty Son of Man rescues his people, not through a military victory, but by dying in their place on the cross. There could not be a more powerful example of humble service. We are called to follow his example by being willing to be the slaves of others, whatever the cost.

7. The proclaimed kingdom – the King's mission

Jesus is God's King; he is enthroned at the right hand of his Father in heaven. But most people do not accept his rule and much is still wrong with the world. God's kingdom has come in Christ, but it has not yet fully come. The fall has still not yet been reversed.

We must wait until Christ's second coming for all God's promises to be completely fulfilled and for his kingdom to be fully established.[6] In the meantime, God is at work extending his kingdom. He does it in a surprising way: through the proclamation of a message, which is all about Jesus the King. Paul describes the good news he is called to proclaim as

'the gospel he [God] promised beforehand through his prophets in the Holy Scriptures regarding his Son, who as to his human nature was a descendant of David, and who through the Spirit of holiness was declared with power to be the Son of God, by his resurrection from the dead: Jesus Christ our Lord.'
(Romans 1:2–4)

Our task as Christians is to proclaim, to preach, this message about Jesus, the King and Saviour, to all peoples. It is often discouraging work, as many reject what they hear, refusing to submit and trust in his offer of forgiveness. But, however hard it may be, it is worth persevering in evangelism. God sent his Spirit at Pentecost to equip his people for the task and he will ensure that the gospel bears fruit.

Jesus tells three parables in Mark 4 that are all about sowing and seeds. Each of them acknowledges the difficulty of serving Christ in this present age, but encourages us by pointing forward to the age to come.

The Parable of the Sower (Mark 4:1–20) – the problem of wastage

When God's kingdom is proclaimed, the message is not always well received. In this parable much of the seed, representing God's Word, falls on bad soil and does not produce fruit. We know the truth of that from our experience. So much of the gospel seed we sow seems to be wasted, making no lasting difference to the lives of those who receive it. Sometimes we even wonder if it is worth continuing. What is the point of witnessing to our colleagues, organizing a children's holiday club or moving to an unreached area if we can expect so little fruit? But Jesus reminds us that one day there will be a bumper crop. Much seed might land on bad soil but 'others, like seed sown on good soil, hear the word, accept it, and produce a crop – thirty, sixty or even a hundred times what was sown' (v. 20). When we see the great harvest in heaven, we will realize how powerful God's Word really is.

The Parable of the Growing Seed (Mark 4:26–29) – the problem of waiting

Once the farmer sows the seed, he must wait; he cannot make it grow. At times it feels as if nothing is happening, but 'all by itself the soil produces corn – first the stalk, then the ear, then the full grain in the ear' (v. 28), and then, at last, the harvest can be gathered. The same process takes place in evangelism. All we can do is spread the gospel, pointing to God's King and his coming kingdom. We cannot make anyone believe it; that is God's task.

Sometimes it seems that nothing is happening. Perhaps we have faithfully proclaimed the gospel to our friends, youth group or church for months or even years, and yet we can see almost no progress. But one day the fruit of the gospel will be seen, when the harvest comes at the end of time.

The Parable of the Mustard Seed (Mark 4:30–32) – the problem of weakness

The kingdom of God 'is like a mustard seed, which is the smallest seed you plant in the ground' (v. 31). At the moment it looks small and unimpressive. The Lord Jesus is largely ignored and our churches are considered insignificant anachronisms that are unlikely to last long in the modern world. We are received with pity at best; scorn and derision at worst. But, just as the mustard seed grows to become 'the largest of all garden plants' (v. 32), so God's kingdom will extend over everything when Jesus returns.

It is hard being a messenger of God's King. We will often experience the problems of wastage, waiting and weakness, but the message is clear: we must persevere, keeping our eyes fixed on the future when the kingdom of God will fully come.

8. The perfected kingdom – the Lamb on the throne

After a young Christian had read through the book of Revelation, her pastor asked her if she had understood it. She replied, 'I didn't understand a lot of it, but I do know we are going to win.' She had grasped the central message of the book. John was writing at a time of great persecution; it certainly did not look as if Christians were on the winning side. But the visions that the apostle saw assured him that they were.

Revelation belongs to a type of literature known as 'apocalyptic'. It uses symbolism to unveil realities that are usually hidden. Most apocalyptic books in the ancient world focus on a great future victory. But Revelation is different; it speaks of a great past victory. John hears a voice in heaven saying, 'See, the Lion of the tribe of Judah, the Root of David, has triumphed' (Revelation 5:5). We expect him to be a mighty figure, but John continues, 'Then I saw a Lamb, looking as if it had been slain, standing in the centre of the throne' (Revelation 5:6). Jesus is the great King of the tribe of Judah, foretold by Jacob in Genesis 49:10, and the mighty son of David, prophesied by Nathan in 2 Samuel 7:12. He is also the suffering Servant who crushed Satan, as the first hint of the gospel in Genesis 3:15 had said he would, through his death on the cross.

It is the past victory Jesus won on the cross that guarantees the final future victory when all his enemies at last will be destroyed. On that great day, an angel will say, 'The kingdom of the world has become the kingdom of our Lord and of his Christ, and he will reign for ever and ever' (Revelation 11:15). At last God's kingdom has fully come.

Figure 10. The perfected kingdom: Jesus Christ, God's King

How should we live now?

The book of Revelation begins with letters from the Lord Jesus to seven churches. In them he urges the Christians to stand firm in the faith. All of them end with a promise to 'him who over-comes'.[7] Jesus is referring to those who remain faithful to him to the end of their lives. They are the ones who enjoy the fruits of his victory in heaven.

The great appeal of Revelation is that we should be those who 'overcome', living today and for the rest of our lives in the light of Christ's kingship. That meant martyrdom for some in the first century who refused to bow down before an image of the Roman emperor and call him 'my Lord and God'. The challenges may be different for us today, but they will still involve a cost. How will we respond when our boss at work asks us to do something illegal, or our friends urge us to join them in an activity we know is wrong? God calls us to 'overcome' and resist temptation. When that is hard, as it often will be, we should remember the vision John saw of the Lamb sitting on the throne in heaven. Jesus has won the victory. He is already King and it is only a matter of time before he returns to establish his authority fully. It is worth obeying him, whatever the cost. He assures us: 'To him who overcomes, I will give the right to sit with me on my throne, just as I overcame and sat down with my Father on his throne' (Revelation 3:21).

Summary

1. The pattern of the kingdom (*Genesis 1 – 2*)	God is King of creation
2. The perished kingdom (*Genesis 3*)	God's rule is rejected
3. The promised kingdom (*Genesis 12*)	God will rule through a king
4. The partial kingdom (*Exodus – 2 Chronicles*)	God establishes a monarchy in Israel
5. The prophesied kingdom (*Ezra – Malachi*)	A new king will come
6. The present kingdom (*Gospels*)	God's King has come
7. The proclaimed kingdom (*Acts – Revelation*)	The King's mission
8. The perfected kingdom	A Lamb on the throne

Figure 11. The once and future King

Bible study

Psalm 2

How does the world respond to God's king (verses 1–3)?

How was that response seen during the time of the monarchy in Israel?

How was it seen when Jesus was on earth?

How is it seen today?

How does God respond (verses 4–9)?

How are these words fulfilled in Jesus (see Matthew 3:16–17; Acts 1:3; 13:32–33; Hebrews 1:5; Revelation 19:15)?

What is God's appeal to the world (verses 10–12)?

What implications does that have for our evangelism?

What does it mean in practice to:
• 'Fear' the Lord?

• 'Kiss the Son'?

• 'Take refuge in him'?

How does this psalm challenge:
• The way we think about Jesus?

• The way we respond to him?

2 | Naked ape or divine image?
Who am I?

What is a human being? One approach to answering that question is purely scientific. Science can examine the body and work out its constituent parts. It can tell you that your body contains enough water to fill a 10-gallon barrel, fat for 7 bars of soap, carbon for 7,000 pencils, phosphorus for 2,200 match heads and iron for a medium-sized nail. It can report that the average human being, if there is such a person, spends 3.5 years eating and 2.5 years on the phone, sheds 19 kilograms of dead skin and grows 2 yards of nasal hair.[1] Those are fascinating facts, but if we want to find an answer to the question 'Who am I?', we need to go beyond science and the mere observation of our bodies.

My aunt once gave me a curious wooden object. It was not immediately obvious what it was. I could have taken samples, put them under a microscope and then discovered it was made of wood with a small amount of ivory inlaid on top. But my questions would still have remained unanswered. I was not simply interested to know what it was made of; I also wanted to know what it was for. My aunt soon ended my confusion by showing me the original packet, which told me that it was a card holder. When a certain part of the box was pushed, it opened to reveal two compartments that were the perfect size for playing cards.

As with the card box, so it is with human beings. If we are to understand ourselves, it is not enough to place our bodies under microscopes. We also need to discover the mind of our Creator: what did he make us for?

1. The pattern of the kingdom – the image of God

In the opening two chapters of the Bible we see the Creator's design for humanity. We are God's creatures, his image and his stewards.

God's creatures

Stephen Jay Gould is typical of those who take a purely scientific approach: 'If the history of life teaches us any lesson, it is that human beings arose as a kind of glorious, cosmic accident, resulting from the catenation [linking] of thousands of improbable events.'[2] Richard Dawkins agrees: 'We human beings have purpose on the brain. It is a nearly universal delusion', and 'to ask what it is is a silly question'.[3] We are simply survival machines blindly programmed by our 'selfish genes'[4] to perpetuate ourselves. If we are just accidents, Dawkins is absolutely right. There is no point looking for purpose or meaning to life because there is none; but the Bible insists we are not accidents. We are God's creatures, lovingly made by him:

> God created man
>   in his own image,
> in the image of God
>   he created him;
> male and female
>   he created them.
> (Genesis 1:27)

The first account of creation, in Genesis 1, describes God's creation of the whole universe, including human beings on the sixth day. The second account, in Genesis 2, narrows the focus on to humankind within God's creation. The man is created first: 'the LORD God formed the man from the dust of the ground and breathed into his nostrils the breath of life, and the man became a living being' (Genesis 2:7). The woman is created later: 'Then the LORD God made a woman from the rib he had taken out of the man, and he brought her to the man' (Genesis 2:22).

Even those who believe that the Bible is God's infallible Word differ about exactly how to interpret Genesis 1 and 2. Some take these chapters entirely literally and believe, for instance, in an actual six-day period of creation and that the woman was literally made instantaneously from one of Adam's ribs. Others believe that the writer is describing what is true, but is using symbolism to express it. They are happy to accept that God might have used the process of evolution and that there were apelike forebears to human beings, but then at one moment in history he breathed his life into two hominids so that they became *Homo sapiens*, spiritual beings made in the image of God. Those two then became the forebears of all human beings today. There is room for debate on such matters, but what is absolutely clear is the fact that human beings are God's creatures.

God's creation of us means that he has authority over us and our duty towards him is to submit. If you make something, you are in authority over it. When I was six I made a clay pot at school. It was a hideous, distorted object. I have never been any good with my hands. No doubt, when my teacher first saw it, she thought she could not let me take it home; the reputation of the school would be destroyed. She was probably tempted to throw it away, but she had no right. I had made it and it was mine to do with it as I wanted. I could have thrown it away, or tried to sell it; it is amazing what passes for modern art these days. But instead, I did what all good sons do with ugly pots: I gave it to my father. Just as I made the pot and thus had the right to do with it as I wanted, so God made human beings and has authority over us.

We human beings often act as if we made the world and are entirely independent, free to do whatever we wish. But as those who have been created by God, we are dependent on him. We depend on our Creator both for life in the first place and for the continuation of life. Every breath we take is enabled by him. That thought should humble us. We should have the attitude of Isaiah, the prophet, who said,

> O LORD you are our Father.
>   We are the clay, you are the potter;
>   we are all the work of your hand.
> (Isaiah 64:8)

Once we recognize that truth, our duty is clear. We are to stop resisting God and submit to him instead.

God's image

'Darwinian man, though well behaved, is really but a monkey shaved.' The zoologist Desmond Morris agrees with that line from one of the Gilbert and Sullivan operas. He writes, 'There are 193 living species of monkeys and apes. One hundred and ninety-two of them are covered with hair. The exception is a naked ape, self-named *Homo sapiens*.'[5] It is undoubtedly true that we are animals, created by God on the sixth day along with all the other creatures that move along the ground. But we are not simply animals. God has set us apart from the rest of the created order and given us a position of unique dignity. We alone have been made in his image. God said, 'Let us make man in our image, in our likeness' (Genesis 1:26).

We human beings represent God and are like him in a way that no other creature is. The writer is not, of course, referring to physical resemblance, because 'God is spirit' (John 4:24). So where can the image of God in us be seen? The Bible never gives a precise answer to that question but theologians have pointed to many ways in which we reflect God uniquely. They refer, for example, to our moral conscience, self-consciousness and religious impulse. Chimpanzees may share 98.4% of their DNA with humans, but there are still many significant differences between them and us. Sometimes the differences are fundamental. For example, no animal has ever shown any evidence of a religious instinct that prompts it to reach out beyond this world to the transcendent realm. At other times, the differences are of degree. Some animals are capable of rational thought, but even the most advanced do not begin to approach the powers of reasoning that humans possess. Wayne Grudem writes:

> Most eight-year-olds can write an understandable letter to their grandparents describing a trip to the zoo, or can move to a foreign country and learn any other language in the world, and we think it entirely normal. But no animal will ever write such a letter to its grandparents, or give the past, present and future of even one French verb or read a detective story and understand it, or understand the meaning of even one verse from the Bible. Human children do all these things quite readily, and in so doing they show themselves so far superior to the whole animal kingdom that we wonder why people have sometimes thought that we are merely another kind of animal.[6]

In the early years of computers, a university department sent a letter to a student that began: 'Dear 344–28–0430: we have a personal interest in you.'[7] Sometimes we can feel as if we are little more than a statistic or a number, but once we grasp the great truth that we are all made in the image of God, we should realize that none of us is insignificant. All of us, whatever our gender, race, sexual orientation and physical or mental capacity, have great dignity and worth. That dignity is reflected in God's command to Noah:

'Whoever sheds the blood of man,
    by man shall his blood be shed;
for in the image of God
    has God made man.'
(Genesis 9:6)

The fact that we are made in God's image tells us something about our purpose as human beings. As people look at us, they should see something of God. We are designed to reflect him, so that his glory is revealed in us. Our function is to glorify him.

There are mirrors in Winchester Cathedral to enable visitors to admire the magnificent carvings in the roof without straining their necks. The tourists will have missed the point if they leave the Cathedral saying, 'What wonderful mirrors!' They are designed not to draw attention to themselves, but rather to point upwards to the ceiling. We, too, are designed to point away from ourselves. Our purpose is not to bring glory to the human race, but rather to reflect God, in whose image we have been made.

God's stewards

As God's representatives on earth, we have been set above the rest of creation and given responsibility for it. God commands the human race, 'Be fruitful and increase in number; fill the earth and subdue it. Rule over the fish of the sea and the birds of the air and over every living creature that moves on the ground' (Genesis 1:28). That is certainly not a charter for the terrible abuse that human beings have inflicted on God's perfect creation over the years. He is not wiping his hands of the world he has made and saying, 'Now it is over to you, do with it what you want.' God continues to care for the world he created and we are accountable to him for how we treat it.

A friend of mine loaned his CD collection to me when he went away to France for a year. I suppose I could have used the CDs as mini-frisbees or as coasters for my coffee cups, but I knew that Philip was coming back at the end of the year and I would have to return them. They were not mine to do with as I wished; I was just a steward. We too are stewards, responsible before God for the way we treat his world.

Some Christians seem to imply that God's command to the human race to 'fill the earth and subdue it' (Genesis 1:28) is no longer important. 'After all', they say, 'we live after the fall. We know that this present world is passing away. Surely our focus should be on the next world that will last for ever. We can forget about God's "creation ordinance". Our responsibility is to obey the great commission that Jesus gave his disciples: "Go and make disciples of all nations" (Matthew 28:19).' They feel they are only really serving God when they are directly involved in the task of evangelism. That is a misunderstanding. The new command of the Saviour does not replace the old command of the Creator. We should obey both.

We should serve God in all we do. We are certainly to be committed to the task of evangelism, but God is not only interested in our labours for the next world. As the Creator, he wants us to do all we can to serve him here too. God has placed us on this earth and given us roles to play within it. As we fulfil those roles, we contribute to the good order of the world that he has entrusted to us. It will never be a perfect place this side of heaven, but it is our job to make it as good as it possibly can be. Do you see how that gives meaning and purpose to everything? Whether we are going to the office, writing an essay or doing the housework, we are serving the creator God. The doctrine of creation means that we cannot just be concerned with a future world; we are to be concerned with this world too. God has

God's creatures	⟶	we should submit to him
God's image	⟶	we should glorify him
God's stewards	⟶	we should serve him

Figure 12. Human beings in creation

entrusted it to us and calls on us to be faithful stewards who seek to serve him in all we do.

2. The perished kingdom – the image of God marred

Genesis 1 – 2 presents a glorious picture of what humans are like, but it is not the whole truth. We are full of contradictions, capable of much that is good and yet also much that is evil. If you listen to a Beethoven sonata, look at a Michelangelo statue or read about what the New York firefighters did on 9/11, you might conclude that human beings are angels. However, you would come to a very different conclusion if you went to Auschwitz in 1945 or Rwanda in 1994. At times we can behave like angels, but we can also behave like animals. A convincing answer to the question 'What is a human being?' must be able to account for that duality of dignity and depravity. That is what we find in the Bible. As those who have been created in God's image, we are the jewel in the crown of his creation. But the Bible also teaches that we are not as we should be; God's image in us has been marred.

Genesis 3 describes the fall of humanity. Adam and Eve disobey God's clear command and eat from the tree of the knowledge of good and evil. That action speaks of a rebellious decision to turn away from his will and go their own way. The immediate consequences are serious. The two creation commands to the human race to fill the earth and subdue it (Genesis 1:28) are affected directly by God's judgment. It will be agony to obey God's command to fill the earth because child-bearing will be very painful (Genesis 3:16). It will also be painful to obey God's command to subdue the earth, because work will be a struggle (Genesis 3:17). But the greatest penalty Adam and Eve receive is death. They are banished from the Garden and the way back to the tree of life is barred (Genesis 3:23–24). They are spiritually dead, cut off from God, and it is only a matter of time before physical death will follow. Adam and Eve do not fulfil their obligations as God's creatures, his image and his stewards. They fail to submit to God, glorify him or serve him and, as a result, they are under his judgment.

Those terrible consequences for Adam and Eve are not limited to them. What they did has huge repercussions for every human being ever since. Because they sinned, we are all sinners. If we are to know who we are as humans, we need to understand, not just the doctrine of creation, but the doctrine of sin. Sin is original, universal, total and fatal.

Sin is original

Paul says in Romans 5:12: ' . . . sin entered the world through one man [Adam], and death through sin, and in this way death came to all men, because all sinned'. Adam, as the first human being, was the fountainhead for the whole of humanity. He represented the whole human race, so, when he sinned, we all sinned. We are bound up with him. His sin led to the corruption of human nature. We are not to think of ourselves as blank sheets when we are born; innocent neutrals who could go one way or the other. We are born sinful. Just ask your parents and they will tell you how true that is. They did not need to teach you how to sin. We are like those old supermarket trolleys that could never go straight. They always seemed to veer to one side when they were pushed forward. We humans are born with a swerve away from God. We cannot go straight because we are born corrupted. The Bible's point is not so much that all sin and are therefore sinners, but rather that all are sinners and therefore sin. The sins we commit are symptoms of the sinful nature that we share and inherit. Our sinful nature is natural to us and deeply rooted in our hearts.

Sin is universal

This truth follows from the last. If sin is original, it must be universal. Paul writes,

'There is no-one righteous, not even one;
  there is no-one who understands,
  no-one who seeks God.
All have turned away ...'
(Romans 3:10–12)

These are uncomfortable words. We try to get ourselves off the hook by pointing the finger at others, such as Osama bin Laden and Saddam Hussein; they are the evil ones. But God will not let us do that. As we point at others, we find lots of fingers pointing back at us.

During the trial of Adolf Eichmann, the mastermind of the holocaust in Nazi Germany, a Jewish man, who had just given evidence against him, was found weeping in the corridor. His friend asked him, 'Why are you crying?' The man replied, 'Because I realize now that he is just a man like I am. I could have done what he did.' He had imagined some awful monster but, when he saw Eichmann right in front of him, he realized that the Nazi was just a man and the awful truth dawned on him. There are not two categories of people, good and evil. We are all sinful.

Sin is total

Sin does not just affect every individual, it affects every part of every individual's life. If a river is polluted at source, that pollution is found along the whole stretch of the river. In the same way, our original sin flows into every aspect of our personality. The theologians call this truth 'total depravity'. That does not mean we are as depraved as we could possibly be, but rather that every part of us is marked by sin; our thinking, emotions, sexuality and speech. Even our good actions are tainted by sin, so that in God's sight 'our righteous acts are like filthy rags' (Isaiah 64:6). If all parts of our personality are corrupted by sin, our wills are included. The Bible teaches, not simply that we do not obey God, but that we cannot: 'the sinful mind is hostile to God. It does not submit to God's law, nor can it do so' (Romans 8:7). Jesus said, 'Everyone who sins is a slave to sin' (John 8:34). We are addicts.

Sin is fatal

The sin of Adam and Eve led to expulsion from the Garden and ever since all their descendants have lived outside Eden, separated from God. We are born under the sentence of death: '... sin entered the world through one man, and death through sin, and in this way death came to all men, because all sinned' (Romans 5:12). We are by nature 'dead' in our 'trespasses and sins' (Ephesians 2:1). Our natural state as those descended from Adam is to be separated from God, under his judgment, facing an eternity apart from him.

- *Sin is original*: 'sin entered the world through one man, and death through sin, and in this way death came to all men, because all sinned' (Romans 5:12).
- *Sin is universal*: 'There is no-one righteous, not even one' (Romans 3:10).
- *Sin is total*: 'our righteous acts are like filthy rags' (Isaiah 64:6).
- *Sin is fatal*: 'the wages of sin is death' (Romans 6:23).

Figure 13. Marred by sin

These are solemn truths. We still have great dignity as God's image-bearers, despite the fall (Genesis 9:6; James 3:9); but we are also depraved, spoilt by our sin.

3. The present kingdom – Jesus Christ, the perfect image

It is almost universally accepted that there is something fundamentally wrong with humanity and there have been many attempts to redeem us. Humanism was popular in the early twentieth century. It rejects any concept of God or of a fall, believing that we are basically good. All we need is better education, health-care and social conditions and then we will reach our destiny. But, despite the massive strides in all those areas in the twentieth century, the history of the past few decades has shown conclusively that we are still capable of awful evil.

Many others placed their hopes in Marxism. If only the proletariat could break free from the shackles of bourgeois oppression, then, it was believed, we human beings could enter a brave new world and be the people we were meant to be. But Stalin's massacres, Mao's Cultural Revolution, the fall of the Berlin Wall and the events in Tiananmen Square all proclaimed the collapse of that dream. Far from freeing the human spirit, Marxism was simply another form of slavery.

No philosophy or political system can ever redeem humanity. What we need is a saviour, and that is exactly what God, in his infinite love, has provided. Someone has expressed it well in these words:

> If our greatest need had been information,
> God would have sent us an educator.
> If our greatest need had been money,
> God would have sent us an economist.
> If our greatest need had been technology,
> God would have sent us a scientist.
> But our greatest need was forgiveness
> So God sent us a saviour.[8]

It was through one man, Adam, that humanity was corrupted and it is through one man, the God-man Jesus Christ, that humanity is restored. Jesus has undone what Adam did. He is the second Adam, the perfect human being.

> O loving wisdom of our God!
>   When all was sin and shame,
> a second Adam to the fight
>   And to the rescue came.[9]

Jesus Christ relived Adam's life

Adam was created in the image of God, but he disobeyed. As a result, God's image has been marred in all Adam's descendants, with one exception. As the divine Son of God, Jesus is the perfect image of God, perfectly reflecting his Father's glory. 'He is the image of the invisible God' (Colossians 1:15). 'The Son is the radiance of God's glory and the exact representation of his being' (Hebrews 1:3).

Jesus was born without the marks of original sin. He was, in that sense, like Adam before the fall, a perfect human. But wonderfully, unlike Adam, he never fell. Where Adam sinned, Christ obeyed. His whole life was one of obedience. He was tempted in the desert after his baptism. 'Go on,' said the devil, 'turn these stones into bread … Throw yourself down from the top of the temple. God will look after you … Do you see all the kingdoms in the world and their splendour? I'll give them to you if you worship me' (see Matthew 4:1–11). When Adam heard the tempting voice of Satan, he yielded and disobeyed God, but Jesus resisted, saying, 'It is written …' (Matthew 4:4, 7, 10). He quoted God's Word and obeyed it. Whereas Adam had sinned, trying to make himself equal with God, Christ obeyed: he 'did not consider equality with God something to be grasped', or 'clung on to' (Philippians 2:6). He was prepared to be obedient to his calling whatever the cost:

> he humbled himself
>> and became obedient to death –
>> even death on a cross!
> (Philippians 2:8)

So Christ lived as Adam should have lived. He is the true human being, God's perfect image.

For Christ to save us, however, it is not enough for him simply to live the perfect life. When the expert on a TV game show produces a magnificent iced cake or performs an elaborate Morris dance, he does not thereby enable the contestants to do the same. His brilliance serves only to magnify their incompetence. The same is true of Jesus' life of obedience. On its own it cannot save us. It rather condemns us by pointing out how far we fall short. It was not enough for Jesus to relive Adam's life; he also had to die Adam's death.

Jesus died Adam's death

As those who have rebelled against God, we all deserve the penalty of death. But Jesus' totally obedient life meant that he was uniquely qualified to be the Saviour. He did not deserve death for his own sins, and so he was able to face it in the place of others.

In Romans 5:12–21 Paul compares and contrasts Adam and Christ. He assumes they are both historical and representative figures. We are familiar with the concept of a representative from the story of David and Goliath. They each acted as the champion of their people, fighting not just for themselves, but for their nations. When David won, Israel won. In a similar way, Adam and Christ are representative of two kinds of humanity.

Adam represents sinful humanity. When he sinned, sin and death followed for all his descendants. 'Consequently ... the result of one trespass was condemnation for all men' (Romans 5:18). By contrast, Jesus is the head of a new kind of humanity. His death on the cross was the final righteous act that crowned a whole life of obedience to his Father's will. As a result, he opened up the possibility for sinful humans to receive justification and life instead of condemnation and death: ' ... the result of one act of righteousness was justification that brings life for all men' (Romans 5:18); ' ... through the obedience of the one man the many will be made righteous' (Romans 5:19). He counteracted the effects of the fall. Because Jesus identified with sinful humanity and faced the penalty we deserved, we no longer need to face it. Instead, we can be accepted by God as those who are perfectly righteous in his sight.

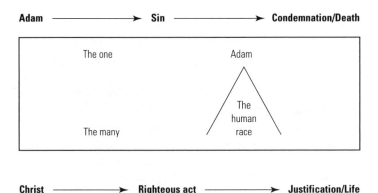

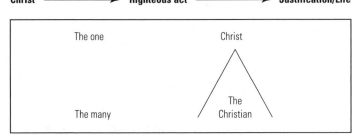

Figure 14. Romans 5:19

Jesus fulfilled Adam's destiny

> Christ has indeed been raised from the dead, the firstfruits of those who have fallen asleep. For since death came through a man, the resurrection of the dead comes also through a man. For as in Adam all die, so in Christ all will be made alive. But each in his own turn: Christ, the firstfruits; then, when he comes, those who belong to him.'
>
> (1 Corinthians 15:20–23)

Having taken our humanity into himself and faced our death, Jesus has been raised and has ascended to the right hand of God. He now reigns with his Father in heaven. He is what Adam should have been: God's image glorifying his Father by perfectly reflecting him, and God's steward, ruling over creation on his Father's behalf. In a sense, he is in the position that Adam was in before the fall. That should give us great hope. It means that our representative, Christ, is back where we belong.

One of my earliest memories is of seeing Neil Armstrong take the first human steps on the moon and hearing his words: 'That's one small step for a man, one giant leap for mankind!' He saw the significance, not just for himself, but for the whole of humanity. There is a famous picture of him and Buzz Alldrin standing triumphantly by an American flag. Likewise the ascension of Jesus into heaven has implications, not just for him as one man, but for the whole of humanity. He has planted the human flag in the presence of God on our behalf. He is there for us. He is the pioneer who has blazed the trial that others can then follow.

By his sin Adam introduced death to humanity, but Christ has opened up the possibility of life by his act of obedience. He has shown that it is possible to come through death and God's condemnation, and then out the other side. Because he died, facing God's judgment in our place, we need not face it and can live for ever. Adam dragged us all down, but Christ came to raise us back up to his Father and to the destiny for which we were created: as God's image and stewards.

4. The proclaimed kingdom – the image restored in Christ

The great Reformer, John Calvin, wrote: 'As long as Christ remains outside us and we are separated from him, all that he has suffered and done for the salvation of the human race remains useless and of no value to us.'[10] We can benefit from Jesus' life, death, resurrection and ascension only when we become part of his new humanity by being joined to him. We must be 'in Christ'.

The expression, 'in Christ' appears 164 times in Paul's letters. It speaks of being united and bound up with him. We will never become fully human again by starting a diet, joining a gym or adopting a new philosophy. The only way to become a true human being is through union with the perfect man, the Lord Jesus Christ.

The close and intimate relationship between Christ and his people is expressed in some striking images in Scripture. Jesus likens himself to a vine, and his disciples to its branches: 'I am the vine; you are the branches. If a man remains in me and I remain in him, he will bear much fruit' (John 15:5). Paul speaks of Christ as the head, and his people as the body: 'he is the head of the body, the church' (Colossians 1:18). He also likens the relationship between a husband and wife to that between Christ and his church (Ephesians 5:22–33). Most strikingly of all, in John 17 Jesus prays that Christians may enjoy as close a relationship with himself and his Father as he enjoys with the Father within the Godhead. We are bound up with, and somehow brought into relationship within, the Trinity.

All those different models speak of a profound and deep personal relationship between Christ and his followers. 'As a branch is united to the tree, and a limb is united to the body, as husband and wife are united to one another, as the Father and Son are united in the Trinity, so the Christian is united to Jesus Christ.'[11]

No-one is born a Christian. If you are a Christian today, it is because you have been converted. You may or may not be able to name the date when that happened. It does not matter very much if you know when your birthday is, as long as you know you have been born, or born again. Whatever the day, it was a momentous one: the day of your death and birth, your funeral and birthday all rolled together. Your old self died and a new self was born.

Paul writes: 'Don't you know that all of us who were baptised into Christ Jesus were baptised into his death? We were therefore buried with him through baptism into death in order that, just as Christ was raised from the dead through the glory of the Father, we too may live a new life' (Romans 6:3–4). 'Baptism' is synonymous with conversion in Paul's thought at this point.

The astonishing language he uses is made possible because we are united or joined to Christ at conversion. Conversion is not just an intellectual recognition that Christ died for me, followed by the receipt of a certificate of forgiveness from him, before I continue to live as before. Christ has not just done something *for* me, he has done something *in* me. Justification and regeneration belong together. God does not simply justify me, declaring me righteous in his sight. He also regenerates me. When I became a Christian, the Holy Spirit entered my life and bound me to Christ. I am regenerated, born again.

By nature we are all joined to Adam; we are 'in Adam'. His sin brought sin and death to every one of us; but Christ, the perfect human being, undid what Adam did. He was not born in Adam, but was a new kind of human being. He relived Adam's life, died Adam's death and fulfilled Adam's destiny. He is at the right hand of God, bringing eternal glory to his Father. And, wonderfully, if we trust in him, we are united to him by the Spirit.

A baby might visit America, go up the Eiffel Tower and take a day trip to Bognor even before he is born, because he is united to his mother in the womb. Wherever she goes, he goes with her, and if we put our trust in Christ, we are in him. What has happened to him has happened to us.

We have died with Christ

If we are united with Christ, our old sinful nature has been crucified with him: 'Christ died for us' (Romans 5:8). He took the penalty for all our sins so that we need not face it ourselves. The old nature may live on in our experiences, but it is on borrowed time. In God's sight we are new people. We have nothing to fear on judgment day because Christ has already been judged in our place.

We have been raised with Christ

'We were therefore buried with him through baptism into death in order that, just as Christ was raised from the dead through the glory of the Father, we too may live a new life' (Romans 6:4). Jesus' resurrection was his justification: God's declaration that he is not under condemnation. We, too, can share in his justification and enter into a relationship with God, confident that we have been justified, redeemed and adopted into his family. That is not because of anything we have done, but because we are in Christ. Paul tells us to 'count [our]selves dead to sin but alive to God in Christ Jesus' (Romans 6:11).

5. The perfected kingdom – the image glorified

As those who have been united to Christ in his life, death, resurrection and ascension, 'our citizenship is in heaven' (Philippians 3:20). That is where we belong. In fact, spiritually speaking, we are there already. 'God raised us up with Christ and seated us with him in the heavenly realms in Christ Jesus' (Ephesians 2:6). But we are not physically there yet. We live in the intersection between the old age of rebellion against God and the new age of God's kingdom. God's Spirit lives within us and has united us to Christ, giving us a new nature with new desires to please God. But the old Adamic nature is not dead yet. We still know the powerful tug of sin in our lives and often fall. There is a constant

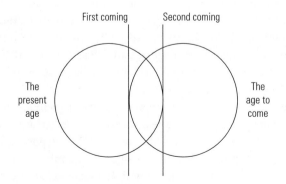

Figure 15. The kingdom, now and not yet

battle in our hearts: 'For the sinful nature desires what is contrary to the Spirit, and the Spirit what is contrary to the sinful nature. They are in conflict with each other' (Galatians 5:17). But that battle will not go on for ever. God is determined to complete the restoration of his new humanity in Christ.

When Christ returns, he will raise his people physically to join him in the new creation. Then, at last, we will fulfil our destiny as humans and be renewed in the likeness of Christ: '. . . we know that when he appears, we shall be like him, for we shall see him as he is' (1 John 3:2). 'And just as we have borne the likeness of the earthly man [Adam], so shall we bear the likeness of the man from heaven' (1 Corinthians 15:49).

How should we live now?

We should be holy people

Paul's discussion in Romans 6 is triggered by the question in verse 1: 'What shall we say, then? Shall we go on sinning, so that grace may increase?' The apostle's immediate response is strong and clear. 'By no means! We died to sin; how can we live in it any longer?' (v. 2). He is speaking not of the impossibility of sin for the Christian, but rather of its incongruity and incompatibility. A teacher might remind a newly appointed prefect, 'Remember your position. You should not smoke now. It is inappropriate.' Paul is saying something similar in Romans 6: sin is completely inappropriate for the Christian. We are new people in Christ, so we should live new lives. Paul urges us, 'Do not offer the parts of your body to sin, as instruments of wickedness, but rather offer yourselves to God' (Romans 6:13).

When Martin Luther was tempted, he used to remind himself, 'I am a baptised person.' He was thinking of the great truths of Romans 6. How can I keep telling lies, looking at pornography, spreading gossip or getting drunk when I remember who I am? I am united to Christ. In him I am 'dead to sin and alive to God' (Romans 6:11) and I should live in a way that reflects those truths.

God's goal for us in eternity is to conform us 'to the likeness of his Son' (Romans 8:29). Do not listen to those who imply that we are diminished as people by our Christian faith. The opposite is true. The more holy we become, the more human we are, as we increasingly conform to the image of Christ, the perfect human being. God has begun that process in this life: 'And we, who with unveiled faces all reflect the Lord's glory, are being transformed into his likeness with ever-increasing glory, which comes from the Lord, who is the Spirit' (2 Corinthians 3:18).

We should be hopeful people

It is easy to despair as we think of the state of humanity in the world. For all the advances of the past few centuries, human nature remains deeply flawed. We may also feel depressed when we think of the state of our own lives. We seem to make so little progress as we keep on falling for the same sins over and over again. But in the midst of all this frustration, we should be people of hope. Christ is the firstborn of a new humanity. He has broken through death and come out the other side, planting the human flag at the right hand of his Father in heaven. It is only a matter of time before he returns to collect us, so that we might join him there. 'When Christ, who is your life, appears, then you also will appear with him in glory' (Colossians 3:4). Despite our perfect creation, we humans are profoundly marred because of our sin. And yet God is still committed to restoring us; that is why he sent his Son Jesus to die for us on the cross. Nothing could proclaim his love more eloquently. It was William Temple, a former Archbishop of Canterbury, who said, 'My worth is what I am worth to God; and that is a marvellous great deal, for Christ died for me.'[12]

The story is told of a man who spent many hours making a beautiful model boat. When it was finished, he enjoyed floating it on the river. One day, however, the wind blew it downstream and he lost it. Months later, he was passing a second-hand shop when he saw his boat in the window. He went in and paid for it. As he held it in his hands, he said to himself, 'Now you're doubly mine. I made you and I bought you.' We human beings also owe a double allegiance to God. In his great love he created us and then, when we were lost in our sin, he sent his Son to pay the price so that we might be restored to a right relationship with him. Such great love demands our gratitude, worship and obedience.

Summary

1. The pattern of the kingdom (*Genesis 1 – 2*)	The image of God
2. The perished kingdom (*Genesis 3*)	The image of God marred
3. The present kingdom (*Gospels*)	Jesus Christ, the perfect image
4. The proclaimed kingdom (*Acts – Revelation*)	The image restored in Christ
5. The perfected kingdom	The image glorified

Figure 16. Naked ape or divine image: who are we?

Bible study

Psalm 8 and Hebrews 2:5–18

Psalm 8
What prompts the psalmist's praise (verses 1–2)?

What do we learn about humanity (verses 3–9)?

How does this reflect what is taught in Genesis 1 – 2?

What implications do these truths have for our relationship with:
• God?

• The rest of creation?

Hebrews 2:5–18
Why are the creation purposes of God for humanity not currently fulfilled (verse 8)?

What has gone wrong?

What hope is there (verses 9–18)?

In what way does Jesus fulfil God's purposes for the whole human race (verse 9)?

How does what he did make any difference to us?

Why did he have to share our humanity?

What has he achieved on our behalf?

What implications should these truths have for:
• How we live now?

• Our attitude to the future?

• Our response to Jesus?

Is a perfect marriage possible?

On a typical Saturday in high summer about 8,000 British couples get married. They spend £1,000 on both the dress and the photographs, £25 per head on food and £30 for each bottle of champagne. The average wedding costs £13,273, which explains why the marriage industry is worth an estimated £4.5 billion a year.[1]

Many people in Britain still believe in marriage, and dream of the perfect wedding day followed by a lifetime of wedded bliss. But increasing numbers believe those dreams belong to the fictional world of 'Mills and Boon' romances. In a recent survey, 40% of engaged couples said they did not expect their marriages to last.[2] We can understand why. A 1999 report showed that the average British marriage lasts 510 weeks.[3] One romantic novel supposedly ended with an unfortunate misprint: 'They got married and lived happily even after.' That mistake is, sadly, often more in tune with reality than what the author intended to write.

So are we faced with a straight choice between the world of reality on the one hand, full of broken dreams and scarred people, and the dream-world of films and cheap novels on the other, where beautiful couples fall in love and live happily ever after? The Bible says 'no'. It gives us both. It certainly does not hide from reality. The world of the Bible is full of sin, unfaithfulness and betrayal; and yet it also points to a relationship of unique intimacy that can never be broken by divorce or death; it is a marriage truly made in heaven.

The focus of this chapter is the relationship of God and his people. As we will see, it is not referred to as a marriage until some way into the Bible, but the image becomes increasingly important until it reaches its culmination with the description of the heavenly marriage of the Lamb in the book of Revelation. But we should not think of this marriage simply as an image that has been imported from human relationships to help us understand spiritual realities. The apostle Paul assumes that the archetypal marriage is between Christ and his people and not the human relationship between a man and a woman. 'Human marriage is not the reality for which Christ and the church provide a sermonic illustration, but the reverse. Human marriage is the earthly type, pointing towards the heavenly reality.'[4] Once we understand the nature of the marriage between God and his people, it will have profound implications for how we relate both to him and to one another.

1. The pattern of the kingdom – human intimacy with God in the Garden

God's love for humanity shines out of the creation accounts in Genesis. He provides for their every need. And his concern is not simply functional. The trees in the Garden do not just produce fruit to keep them alive; they are also 'pleasing to the eye' (Genesis 2:9). The woman created as a companion for Adam delights him so much that he writes the first poem to celebrate

(Genesis 2:23). But the central feature is not the relationship of Adam and Eve with each other, but their relationship with God. His presence with them is symbolized by the tree of life in the middle of the Garden. Like them, it is only when we enjoy relationship with him that we experience life as it was designed to be lived. Jesus said in a prayer to his heavenly Father, 'Now this is eternal life: that they may know you, the only true God, and Jesus Christ, whom you have sent' (John 17:3).

2. The perished kingdom – human beings are banished from God's presence

The perfect relationship Adam and Eve enjoyed with God is broken by their disobedience. He still comes close to them, 'walking in the garden in the cool of the day' (Genesis 3:8), but they hide from him in their shame. His continuing tender love for them is revealed when he makes clothes for them to hide their nakedness (3:21), but he must still judge them. They are banished from the Garden and a guard is placed to prevent them from returning to the tree of life (3:24).

3. The promised kingdom – 'I will be your God and you will be my people'

God is determined to restore the relationship between himself and humanity. The rest of the Bible has been described as unfolding 'the drama of a loving God winning back to himself "a pure bride for her one husband" '.[5] That drama begins with God making promises to Abraham. His descendants will become a nation and will be greatly blessed (Genesis 12:1–3). God chooses the Israelites to be set apart from the other nations as those who belong uniquely to him. That relationship is often expressed in a repeated refrain: 'I will be their God and they will be my people' (Jeremiah 31:33;

cf. Genesis 17:8; Ezekiel 11:20; 37:23, 27; 2 Corinthians 6:16; Hebrews 8:10).

4. The partial kingdom – God's covenant relationship with Israel

A marriage ceremony

A covenant is a formal, binding agreement between two parties. God enters into a covenant with Abraham and his descendants when he promises to bless them (Genesis 12:1–3; 17:1–14). They are his people simply because of his gracious choice, which is not based on any merits of theirs. God acts in accordance with his promises to Abraham when he rescues the Israelites from slavery in Egypt. He then reveals his law to Moses on Mount Sinai, making it clear what the Israelites' obligations are within their covenant relationship with him. They are his people by grace alone, but they will have to obey his law if they want to enjoy blessing within the covenant (Exodus 19:5).

When Moses comes down from the mountain, he calls on the people to accept their covenant obligations. He builds an altar, which represents God's presence, and he sets up twelve stone pillars, which stand for the twelve tribes of Israel. Both parties to the agreement are thus symbolically present. Some animals are then sacrificed and their blood is sprinkled before God on the altar. The blood is a powerful demonstration of the incompatibility that exists between a holy God and a sinful people. They can enjoy a relationship with him only if something is done about their sin; blood must be shed. Moses then reads God's law to the people from 'the book of the covenant'. They respond, 'We will do everything the LORD has said; we will obey' (Exodus 24:7). 'Moses then took the blood, sprinkled it on the people and said, "This is the blood of the covenant that the LORD has made with you in accordance with all these words"' (24:8). It seems that the blood has a twofold significance. It brings assurance of atonement, reminding the people of the sacrifice the Lord has accepted to satisfy his wrath against their sin. But it is likely that it contains a more solemn message as well. It commits them to keeping the covenant on pain of death.

It is hardly surprising that the prophets regularly came to refer to the covenant that was ratified at Sinai in marital terms. The occasion described in Exodus 24 has much in common with a marriage ceremony. Two parties are committing themselves to one another in an exclusive relationship. The Lord has already declared his love for Israel as his holy people, set apart from all the other tribes and nations of the earth. Now the people bind themselves to him. Just as a human couple 'forsake all others', so Israel agrees to God's commandments, all of which flow from the first: 'You shall have no other gods before me' (Exodus 20:3).

The marital home

As soon as the covenant is ratified, Moses returns up the mountain and receives detailed instructions about how to build the tabernacle (Exodus 25 – 31). The marital home is soon to be built. God, the divine husband, is coming to live among his people. This is the great goal to which the whole book has been heading. The purpose of the exodus from Egypt and the giving of the law is that the Lord and his people might enjoy fellowship with one another. God's law makes it clear that there can be no easy intimacy between the holy God and sinful people. Priests must act as intermediaries and offer sacrifices, but still the Israelites will enjoy access to God that is open to no other people. Expectations are high; but they are soon dashed. At the very moment when Moses is on the mountain being told how to build the tabernacle, the people down below are already showing their unfaithfulness by building a golden calf.

Just days after they have vowed to obey all the Lord's commands, the Israelites disobey the first two. They are no longer worshipping God alone and they are making an idol. Their behaviour puts the whole future of the covenant relationship in doubt. How can God live among them now? He is furious and declares his intention to destroy them, but Moses intercedes for them. God graciously relents and the covenant is reaffirmed. The tablets of stone, that were broken when Moses came down from the mountain and saw the people's sin, are replaced and the plans for the tabernacle are repeated (Exodus 35 – 40). God will live with his people after all.

A jealous God

When the Lord reaffirms the covenant, he calls on the people to obey him in the future. In particular, they are not to enter into an agreement with those who live in the land he is giving to them, lest they then be led astray by them and begin to worship their gods. The Lord demands exclusive allegiance: 'Do not worship any other god, for the LORD, whose name is Jealous, is a jealous God' (Exodus 34:14). Just as a man will not share his wife with another, so the Lord will not tolerate his people worshipping any other god.

Spiritual prostitution

The very personal nature of the relationship between God and his people is confirmed by the term that is used to speak of the sin of idolatry. It is nothing less than prostitution. God warns the people:

'Be careful not to make a treaty with those who live in the land; for when they prostitute themselves to their gods and sacrifice to them, they will invite you and you will eat their sacrifices. And when you choose some of their daughters as wives for your sons and those daughters prostitute themselves to their gods, they will lead your sons to do the same.'
(Exodus 34:15–16)

'Prostitution' is a shocking term that expresses the horror of the sin of a people who have been specially chosen to belong to

God. Raymond Ortlund has written an excellent book, originally entitled *Whoredom*, that follows the theme of God's unfaithful wife through Scripture. He begins, 'The title of this book offends its author. Doubtless it offends the reader as well. But in light of the biblical story to be surveyed in this volume the appropriateness of the title will become obvious. And so it stands, as offensive as is the sin to which it refers.'[6] That sin is not limited to idolatry. Any time God's people follow 'the lusts of their own hearts and eyes', they are committing the sin of spiritual prostitution (Numbers 15:39).

God is in no doubt about what will happen in the future. He speaks to Moses just before he dies and the people enter the land:

> 'You are going to rest with your fathers, and these people
> will soon prostitute themselves to the foreign gods of the
> land they are entering. They will forsake me and break the
> covenant I made with them. On that day I will become angry
> with them and forsake them; I will hide my face from them,
> and they will be destroyed.'
> (Deuteronomy 31:16–17)

The Israelites do enjoy much blessing in the land, despite their sin. God lives in their midst in the temple, and they benefit greatly from his presence with them; but it is only a matter of time before he must judge them for their unfaithfulness.

The king's marriage

An estimated three quarters of a billion people in 55 countries watched the wedding of Prince Charles and Lady Diana Spencer. Everyone loves a wedding, especially a royal wedding. Psalm 45 was written for a similar occasion; possibly the marriage of Solomon.

But the language used points beyond that historical event to the marriage of a king far greater than any merely human king. He is described in the most exalted terms possible:

Your throne, O God, will last for ever and ever;
    a sceptre of justice will be the sceptre of your kingdom.
You love righteousness and hate wickedness;
    therefore God, your God, has set you above your
        companions
    by anointing you with the oil of joy.
(Psalm 45:6–7)

This divine king is united to a bride with whom he is captivated. The psalmist tells her, 'The king is enthralled by your beauty' (v. 11). Then, having been prepared for the wedding, 'In embroidered garments she is led to the king' (v. 14).

This psalm looks ahead to a time when the intimacy between God and his people will far surpass what the people are currently enjoying, even in the days when Israel's history is at its height. The writer to the Hebrews reveals that it speaks of the Lord Jesus (Hebrews 1:8–9). He is the king who is far greater even than Solomon. It follows that the bride with whom he is 'enthralled' is his people. No human marriage, however good, can compare with such a relationship.

It is no wonder that many Christians cannot help reading Solomon's great love poem, the Song of Songs, without thinking of their relationship with Christ. It is probably a mistake to read it as an allegory. We should take it at face value, as a celebration of love, romance and sexual intimacy in a human marriage. But now that Christ has come, we know that the longings that are partially fulfilled in the marriage of a man and a woman are fully met only in a union with Christ.

5. The prophesied kingdom – God's marriage with his people will be renewed

What is implicit in the earlier books of the Old Testament is made explicit in the prophetic books. God's covenant with his people is often described as a marriage. It forms the basis of the coming judgment that is the dominant theme of the prophecies. God, the jealous husband, must punish his people for their prostitution. But the marriage is also the basis of great hope. God is a loving husband who will remain faithful to his marriage vows. The judgment will bring discipline, but not divorce.

Hosea: a tale of two marriages

Hosea was active in the northern kingdom of Israel in the eighth century BC. He receives an extraordinary command from God right at the start of his prophetic ministry. The Jerusalem Bible captures the shock of it: 'Go marry a whore and get children with a whore for the country itself has become nothing but a whore by abandoning God' (Hosea 1:2).

I imagine an old friend looking forward to his first meeting with Hosea's wife, Gomer. What will she be like? No doubt she is a keen believer like him; a great support in his ministry. But, as she enters the house, the friend can't help noticing that she is wearing a risqué mini-skirt and that the make-up is rather overdone, but he tells himself that he should not judge by appearances and pushes those first impressions out of his mind. A little later he manages to engage her in conversation and asks, 'So, Gomer, what line of work were you in when you met Hosea?' He is not prepared for the answer. 'I was in prostitution, actually,' she says, without a hint of a blush. He cannot believe it. How could such a godly man have married a woman like her? He asks Hosea to explain himself and he is told, 'God told me to do it. My marriage to Gomer represents God's marriage to Israel. Every time the people hear of her latest infidelities, they are receiving a message from God. He is confronting them with the awful way in which they treat him. Just as Gomer is unfaithful to me, so Israel is unfaithful to him and he must judge them.'

Gomer leaves Hosea and sets up home with another man, but God tells him, 'Go, show your love to your wife again, though she is loved by another and is an adulteress. Love her as the LORD loves the Israelites, though they turn to other gods and love the sacred raisin cakes' (3:1). Hosea obeys God's command, even suffering the indignity of having to pay his wife's lover to let her go (3:2). His commitment to the marriage, despite the way in which Gomer behaves, points towards God's amazing grace in his dealings with his people. Although they must be punished for their sin, that judgment will not signal the end of the marriage. In fact, God will use it as a means of wooing his wife back to him (see 2:14). He longs that she will come to her senses and say, 'I will go back to my husband as at first, for then I was better off than now' (2:7).

The coming judgment is proclaimed through the names God gives to Hosea's children: 'Jezreel' (a place of infamy in Israel's history), 'Not loved' and 'Not my people' (1:4–9). But there is still hope beyond the judgment. God promises,

'I will show my love to the one I called
    "Not my loved one".
I will say to those called "Not my people",
    "You are my people";
  and they will say, "You are my God".'
(2:23)

The apostle Peter tells us that those promises are fulfilled in the church. Writing to a mixed group of Jewish and Gentile believers, he says, 'Once you were not a people, but now you are the people of God; once you had not received mercy, but now you have received mercy' (1 Peter 2:10). God's marriage with his people has been renewed in Christ.

Jeremiah: the new covenant
Jeremiah prophesied in the southern kingdom of Judah in the seventh century BC, about one hundred years after Hosea. He also speaks of the spiritual adultery of the people:

'If a man divorces his wife
   and she leaves him and marries another man,
should he return to her again?
   Would not the land be completely defiled?
But you have lived as a prostitute with many lovers –
   would you now return to me?'
declares the LORD.
(Jeremiah 3:1)

God invites his people to apply the principles of his law to their behaviour. They know that it is inconceivable for a husband to have his wife back after she has been guilty of sexual sin and has then married someone else (Deuteronomy 24:1–4). So how can God have them back after the way they have behaved? The implication seems to be that God and his people are divorced. There appears to be no hope at this stage of Jeremiah's ministry. But, once again, the marriage relationship, which is the ground of judgment, is also the ground of hope. God must judge his people for their disobedience to his covenant stipulations; and yet he must also be faithful to his covenant promises. He will achieve this by inaugurating a new covenant.

In most broken relationships both parties are at least partly to blame; but there is only one guilty party in the disintegration of the old covenant. God says, 'they broke my covenant, though I was a husband to them' (31:32). And yet, despite that betrayal, he remains committed to fulfilling his original covenant promises. He pledges to introduce a new covenant. At its heart will be a renewed relationship of intimacy with his people, which cannot be spoiled by their sin:

'This is the covenant that I will make
      with the house of Israel
      after that time . . .
I will put my law in their minds
   and write it on their hearts.

I will be their God
   and they will be my people.
No longer will a man teach his neighbour,
   or a man his brother, saying, "Know the LORD,"
because they will all know me,
   from the least of them to the greatest . . .
For I will forgive their wickedness
   and will remember their sins no more.'
(Jeremiah 31:33–34)

Ezekiel: an ungrateful wife

Ezekiel lived as an exile in Babylon at the beginning of the sixth century BC. He uses a number of powerful methods to communicate his message, including allegory.

Israel is likened to a baby abandoned at birth: unwashed, unloved and with its umbilical cord uncut. God has mercy on her and saves her life. Time passes and she grows to maturity. As God passes by one day he notices her: ' . . . when I looked at you and saw that you were old enough for love, I spread the corner of my garment over you and covered your nakedness. I gave you my solemn oath and entered into a covenant with you' (16:8). She is in a pitiful state, naked and covered in blood, but he bathes her and adorns her with beautiful clothes. She becomes famous throughout the world for her beauty. It is a classic tale of rags to riches and God must take all the credit; she would be nothing without him. But if God did everything to establish the marriage, it is his wife who acts alone in destroying it. The story takes a sudden turn for the worse: 'But you trusted in your beauty and used your fame to become a prostitute. You lavished your favours on anyone who passed by' (16:15).

How could she have done it? Adultery is always wicked, but we can at least understand it when the spouse has been cruel and unreasonable. But this husband could not have been more loving; and yet still his wife spurned him and went promiscuously after other lovers. God's comment is surely an understatement: 'Such things should not happen, nor should they ever occur' (16:16). His judgment is inevitable after the way his people have behaved. He says,

> 'I will sentence you to the punishment of women who commit adultery and who shed blood; I will bring upon you the blood vengeance of my wrath and jealous anger. Then I will hand you over to your lovers, and they will tear down your mounds and destroy your lofty shrines. They will strip you of your clothes and take your fine jewellery and leave you naked and bare.'
> (16:38–39)

She is back where she began; naked and helpless.

We could understand if that were where the story finishes. There is no happy ending in Ezekiel's other extended allegory in chapter 23 about two adulterous sisters, representing Israel and Judah. But chapter 16 ends on a glorious high note. Despite all the wickedness of his people, God will make sure that the marriage lasts. He assures them: 'Yet I will remember the covenant I made with you in the days of your youth, and I will establish an everlasting covenant with you' (16:60). The marriage still has a future. That hope must have sustained the faithful Israelites during the long days after the exile and their return to the land, while they waited for the time of fulfilment. One day they would enjoy a fully restored relationship with their God.

6. The present kingdom – the bridegroom has come

When the time of fulfilment finally arrives, it is not because the hearts of the people have changed. Jesus refers to his contemporaries as 'a wicked and adulterous generation' (Matthew 12:39; 16:4; Mark 8:38). But God chooses that time to fulfil his covenant promises. He does so by sending his Son to earth.

John the Baptist speaks of himself as the best man whose role is to serve the bridegroom and then recede into the background (John 3:28–30). Jesus uses similar terminology when he addresses John's disciples, who are concerned that Jesus and his followers are not observing the religious duty of fasting. He tells them, 'How can the guests of the bridegroom mourn while he is with them?' That is a time for celebration and feasting. But it will not last for long: 'The time will come when the bridegroom will be taken from them; then they will fast' (Matthew 9:15).

Jesus will not fully restore the covenant on his first visit to earth; at least, not in his people's experience. His death on the cross seals the new covenant (Luke 22:20; Hebrews 10:11–18) and tears down the curtain that had barred his people from entering God's presence. They are now free to approach him without fear (Hebrews 10:19–22). But they will not be able to enjoy all the fruits of their relationship with him until he returns at the end of time, and that may be a long time away. Just as the bridegroom in the Parable of the Ten Virgins was 'a long time in coming' (Matthew 25:5), so there will be a period of delay before Jesus returns. The parable urges us to be ready because that could happen at any time.

7. The proclaimed kingdom – the betrothed is prepared for her wedding

An invitation to a wedding banquet

The bridegroom has come and then gone away again. The great wedding celebration is still in the future. Meanwhile, invitations to the feast are being issued. In the Parable of the Wedding Banquet (Matthew 22:1–14) Jesus describes how those who are first invited, the Jewish people, refuse the invitation, so the king's servants are sent out far and wide to encourage others, the nations, to attend. But standards are still preserved. The guests must wear proper wedding clothes. Christ's people must repent when they come to him.

We live in the age when people from all nations are invited to participate in the royal wedding between Christ and his people. Those who accept do not have to wait to enter into an intimate relationship with Christ. Paul writes, 'I have been crucified with Christ and I no longer live, but Christ lives in me. The life I live in the body, I live by faith in the Son of God, who loved me and gave himself for me' (Galatians 2:20). That union with Christ is profound, but it is not perfect in our experience. As long as we live on earth away from our true home, heaven, where Christ dwells, we must live 'by faith'. We must wait for the final consummation of our union when we finally see him.

The betrothed people of God

Paul uses the language of betrothal to speak of our current position. He is concerned that the Corinthian Christians might be led astray by some new leaders who have emerged, who are undermining his authority in a church that he had been used to establish. He is forced to defend himself, but makes it clear that he does so, not to defend his reputation, but rather out of concern for the Corinthians' spiritual health:

> I am jealous for you with a godly jealousy. I promised you to one husband, to Christ, so that I might present you as a pure virgin to him. But I am afraid that just as Eve was deceived by the serpent's cunning, your minds may somehow be led astray from your sincere and pure devotion to Christ.
> (2 Corinthians 11:2–3)

Like the father of a bride, Paul has betrothed them to Christ, their heavenly husband, and he is determined that they should remain spiritually pure and undefiled until then. That is why he feels bound to protect them against the dangerous teaching of his opponents. We should share Paul's concern. We should do all we can to ensure that we are not corrupted by sin or error so that we are ready for the bridegroom when he comes.

The marriage of Christ and his church

Our responsibility as Christians is to live lives of pure devotion to Christ, our divine husband. That will have implications for every area of life, including our marriages. In Ephesians 5:22–33 Paul instructs Christian husbands and wives how they should relate to one another. We will return to that theme later. Our focus now is Paul's teaching about the nature of the relationship between Christ and his church, which is the foundation of his teaching about human marriage.

Husbands are instructed to love their wives and are pointed to Christ as the model husband they should follow: 'Husbands, love your wives, just as Christ loved the church and gave himself up for her to make her holy, cleansing her by the washing with water through the word, and to present her to himself as a radiant church, without stain or wrinkle or any other blemish, but holy and blameless' (5:25–27). Paul has the same end in view as in 2 Corinthians 11:2–3; the great wedding day when Christ returns. But this time it is Christ himself, rather than the apostle, who is concerned to see that his people are suitably prepared for that day.

Brides go to elaborate lengths and spend large sums of money to ensure they are at their best for their wedding. They will take hours choosing the dress, having their hair done, applying make-up and much else besides. Meanwhile the bridegroom is on the golf course or watching the football on television. He does not take a detailed interest in his fiancée's preparations, partly because convention does not allow it, and partly because his patience is soon exhausted by such things. But the divine bridegroom is very different. He could not have gone further in his efforts to ensure that his people will be perfect on their big day and he could not have paid a higher price; he died to make it possible. There could be no more loving husband. Because of his death for us, we are completely cleansed from sin the moment we respond with faith to the gospel. Paul no doubt has the allegory of Ezekiel 16 in mind, with its story of a girl who is rescued, washed and clothed by the Lord.

Having pointed to the example of Christ as the model husbands should copy in loving their wives, Paul presents another basis for that love: 'husbands ought to love their wives as their own bodies' (Ephesians 5:28). He is referring to the fact that husband and wife are 'one flesh' (Genesis 2:24). But, once again, the ultimate foundation of his teaching is found in the marriage of Christ and the church. 'The Christ/church parallel is not merely illustrative but the generating theological centre of his entire presentation.'[7] Paul writes:

> After all, no-one ever hated his own body, but he feeds and cares for it, just as Christ does the church – for we are members of his body. 'For this reason a man will leave his father and mother and be united to his wife, and the two will become one flesh.' This is a profound mystery – but I am talking about Christ and the church.
> (Ephesians 5:29–32)

Paul is saying that the great statement about marriage in Genesis 2:24, which he quotes, does not simply speak of human marriage. It also refers to the deep union that exists in the relationship between Christ and his people. We are 'one flesh' with him; 'members of his body'. It is for that reason that he cares for us so diligently. 'When the church hurts, Christ her head hurts; when the church grows in grace, Christ rejoices.'[8] Human husbands should exhibit the same care for their wives.

8. The perfected kingdom – the marriage of the Lamb

Sometimes I am not aware that I am hungry until I have a nibble of whatever is being prepared in the kitchen. That is enough to get all the juices going and the stomach rumbling, and it is almost more frustration than I can bear when I am told that I must wait until the mealtime before I can have any more.

We Christians have had a taste of the wonderful experience of knowing Jesus Christ. Sometimes we have felt as if our hearts could almost burst as we sense something of the greatness of his love. But we are not satisfied. We know that we have only begun to paddle in the shallows and that there is so much more of him to be appreciated and enjoyed. We can pray with Paul that we may have the power to grasp more of the width, length, height and depth of his love (Ephesians 3:17–19), but we know that it is a prayer that will never be fully answered in this world. And so the more we know of Christ, the more we realize how little we know and long for that great day when he returns and we will 'know fully' as we are 'fully known' (1 Corinthians 13:12).

John's vision in the book of Revelation tells us what we can expect. He heard a great crowd shouting:

'Hallelujah!
  For our Lord God Almighty reigns.
Let us rejoice and be glad
  and give him glory!
For the wedding of the Lamb has come,
  and his bride has made herself ready.
Fine linen, bright and clean,
  was given her to wear.'
(Revelation 19:6–8)

Christ's goal has been accomplished and his church is wearing the clothes of perfect purity. At last she can come into his presence and enjoy her marriage to the full. John sees

... the Holy City, the new Jerusalem, coming down out of heaven from God, prepared as a bride beautifully dressed for her husband. And I heard a loud voice from the throne

saying, 'Now the dwelling of God is with men, and he will live with them. They will be his people, and God himself will be with them and be their God.'
(Revelation 21:2-3)

Jonathan Edwards, the New England Puritan, has commented:

> Then the church shall be brought to the full enjoyment of her bridegroom, having all tears wiped away from her eyes; and there shall be no more distance or absence. She shall then be brought to the entertainments of an eternal wedding-feast, and to dwell for ever with her bridegroom; yea to dwell eternally in his embraces. Then Christ will give her his love; and she shall drink her fill, yea, she shall swim in the ocean of his love.[9]

The promises that run throughout Scripture and the longings that exist in every human heart will at last be completely fulfilled.

The practical consequences of God's marriage with his people

This great theme of God's marriage with his people has profound implications for the way we should think and act in every area of life.

Implications for our relationship with God

God's love is magnified
The Lord God who made the universe is prepared to call us, not just his creatures, or even his friends, or sons, but his bride. We will probably never fully understand why he should have set his love upon us; it is a mystery of grace. Yet he has, and we should praise him for it with all our hearts and do all we can to delight in him as he delights in us.

My local paper carried a story a while ago about a man who had managed to leave his wife at a petrol station and then drive on for forty miles without noticing. He only realized his mistake when he turned to her and asked her for a toffee. Perhaps that was a symptom of a marriage in trouble. Human marriages so easily decline from warm intimacy into a cold co-existence. The same can happen in our relationship with God.

Perhaps we can look back on times in the past when we revelled in his love but, if we are honest, those days are gone. Our Christian life is now more one of duty than delight. It need not be like that. And what better way to seek to restore the passion than to meditate on the greatness of our divine husband's love to us? There is something very wrong with our hearts if they have not begun to be warmed by the magnificent truths in this chapter. But there is a danger that we too quickly forget them. Let us, rather, resolve to keep them in the forefront of our minds and our hearts.

Our sin is heightened

The closer the relationship we have with someone, the more they can hurt us. The insult of a stranger is soon brushed off, but an argument with a close friend can affect us for days; and the unfaithfulness of a lover creates wounds that can cause intense pain for years. That is the nature of our sin against God. It is not the breaking of an impersonal code, but the betrayal of a loving husband. We think so little of our sin because we think so little of him. But if we really understood his love and all that he has done for us, we would surely beg for his forgiveness and determine to repent.

Princess Diana famously said, 'There were three of us in this marriage so it was a bit crowded.' Is there a third party in our relationship with Christ; some other lover who threatens to replace him at the centre of our lives? It could be some sin we are clinging on to, a relationship or ambition. Or perhaps it is a more general concern to fit in with those around us and not stand out. If so, we need to listen to the words of James: 'You adulterous people, don't you know that friendship with the world is hatred towards God?' (James 4:4). We cannot have two husbands; we must choose. I once received a tragic letter from a friend who decided to put a girlfriend above Christ in his life. He wrote very honestly, 'I can't serve two gods; Sarah is my god.' He saw the issues clearly, but he made the wrong choice. Let us do all we can to turn from the rivals to Christ in our lives.

Implications for human marriage

Married couples should be faithful to one another

God is entirely faithful to his covenant promises to his people and he expects them to be faithful to him in turn; they are to worship him alone. He expects a husband and wife to exhibit the same faithfulness in the covenant relationship of marriage. The prophet Malachi condemns his people for 'breaking faith' with God and not keeping their covenant with him (Malachi 2:10–11). He then immediately condemns them in the same terms for their unfaithfulness in marriage: '... the LORD is acting as the witness between you and the wife of your youth, because you have broken faith with her, though she is your partner, the wife of your marriage covenant' (Malachi 2:14). The God who is faithful to the covenant with his people expects them to be faithful to their covenant with one another. That is why he says, 'I hate divorce' (Malachi 2:16).

The world increasingly thinks little, or nothing, of adultery and divorce. For many, a relationship is based on an emotional bond. If that dies, the marriage is effectively over. A couple should simply face facts and move on. One celebrity recently justified leaving his wife and children by saying, 'It was the most difficult decision I'll ever make ... it would have been a lot easier to have stayed in my marriage, but I had to be true to myself.'[10] A football personality has even gone so far as to blame God for his adultery, saying, 'I am not proud of my record with women. I have always had an appetite to explore the delights of love and lust and, I am afraid, one partner was never going to be enough for me. It was simply the way God made me.'[11]

God will not accept such excuses. We are not animals, incapable of controlling our desires. Those who marry make commitments to one another and God expects them to be kept. He provides the perfect model. He kept his vows to his people, despite their frequent indifference and unfaithfulness to him. Marriage is based on promises, not feelings alone. A marriage may well go through a difficult patch; if so, it should be worked at prayerfully, not abandoned.

There are, of course, many in our churches who have committed adultery or been divorced. They should not feel they have committed the unforgivable sin, or that their lives are unrepairable. God in his grace offers forgiveness and hope to us all. But he also calls on us to live from now on according to his standards.

Married couples should follow the model of Christ and his church
We have seen already that Paul presents the relationship of Christ and his church as a model for Christian couples to apply to their marriages. He begins by addressing the wives: 'Wives, submit to your husbands as to the Lord. For the husband is the head of the wife as Christ is the head of the church, his body, of which he is the Saviour. Now as the church submits to Christ, so also wives should submit to their husbands in everything' (Ephesians 5:22–24). Such language conjures up for many the image of a pathetic woman who never takes any initiative and is a lap-dog for her brutal, domineering husband; always at his beck and call. But that is a long way from what Paul has in mind. Submission does not imply inferiority. The Son submits to the Father in the Godhead, but is fully divine (1 Corinthians 11:3). To submit involves accepting that the husband and wife have different roles in the marriage and that it is the husband who is called to be the loving leader, with ultimate responsibility. Different couples will have different ways of working out what that means in practice, but they are all called to follow

the principle. The wife may well disagree with her husband, and she will no doubt try to persuade him and even plead with him to change his mind, but, in the end, she is called to submit, as the church submits to her husband, Christ.

But a marriage can work as God intended only if both individuals play their part. If the wife's role sounds hard, the husband's is even more demanding. Paul writes, 'Husbands, love your wives, just as Christ loved the church and gave himself up for her to make her holy, cleansing her by the washing with water through the word . . .' (Ephesians 5:25–26). His first concern is not to be for his own interests, but for hers. He is to be prepared to make great sacrifices in order to see her flourish.

A clergyman friend of mine often addresses the groom in his wedding sermon and tells him to jot down the five qualities he most admires about his new wife. He is then encouraged to keep the list and look at it every year on their anniversary. If those qualities are continuing to blossom as the years go by, it is a good sign that he is being a loving husband; but if they are diminishing, he should examine his behaviour towards her.

When Anne Morrow married Charles Lindbergh she was a nervous, shy woman, whereas he was a self-confident hero, known throughout the world as the first man to fly solo across the Atlantic. But she grew in confidence and became, in time, one of America's most popular authors. Towards the end of her life she wrote, 'The sheer fact of finding myself loved was unbeliev-able and changed my world, my feelings about life and myself. I was given confidence, strength, and almost a new character. The man I was to marry believed in me and what I could do, and consequently I found I could do more than I realized.'[12] Love can transform us. We know that from our relationship with Christ. Husbands are called to show the same love to their wives.

Implications for singleness
A large proportion of Christians are single, whether because they have never married or because they are divorced or their spouse

has died. Both Christ and Paul speak positively about singleness (Matthew 19:8–12; 1 Corinthians 7:32–35), none the less, the experience of singleness can be very hard. Some struggle throughout their lives with unfulfilled longings for intimacy; others are left feeling that no-one really cares for them. But Christ brings great comfort. There will be no human marriage in the next world (Matthew 22:30), but he offers to all of us, whether married or single, a perfect marriage with him that will last for eternity.

After I had preached about the marriage of the Lamb in the book of Revelation, one of the great older saints in the church told me, 'I can't wait for my wedding day.' She had been single all her life and was longing to be united with Christ, her heavenly husband. After the great description of the bride being united with Christ, it is no surprise to find these words in the last chapter of the Bible: 'The Spirit and the bride say "Come!"' (Revelation 22:17). If we have begun to understand the wonder of our relationship with Christ, that will be our longing too, whether we are single or married, and we will join in the heartfelt prayer with which the Bible ends, 'Come, Lord Jesus' (Revelation 22:20).

Summary

1. The pattern of the kingdom (*Genesis 1 – 2*)	Adam and Eve enjoy intimacy with God in the Garden
2. The perished kingdom (*Genesis 3*)	Humans banished from God's presence
3. The promised kingdom (*Genesis 12*)	God's promise to Abraham: 'I will be your God and you will be my people'
4. The partial kingdom (*Exodus – 2 Chronicles*)	God's covenant relationship with Israel
5. The prophesied kingdom (*Ezra – Malachi*)	God's marriage with his people will be renewed: Hosea, Ezekiel, Jeremiah
6. The present kingdom (*Gospels*)	The bridegroom has come
7. The proclaimed kingdom (*Acts – Revelation*)	The betrothed people of God, being prepared for her wedding
8. The perfected kingdom	The marriage of the Lamb

Figure 17. God's marriage: is a perfect relationship possible?

⬭ Bible study

Ezekiel 16

Undeserved love (verses 1–14)
What are the parallels with the Israelites?

And with Christians today (see, for example, Ephesians 2:1–10)?

Rejected love (verses 15–34)
How was the Israelites' unfaithfulness seen?

And ours today (see, for example, James 4:1–6)?

Jealous love (verses 35–52)
How was God's judgment on the Israelites expressed?

What do we deserve (see, for example, Romans 2:1–4)?

Forgiving love (verses 53–63)
What does God promise the Israelites?

How have these promises been fulfilled (see, for example, Romans 5:1–11)?

What are the implications of these truths for:
• Our view of God?

• Our understanding of ourselves?

• Our behaviour?

4 | Wealth and possessions
Your money or your life?

Seventeen billion dollars is spent each year in the West on pet food; but only thirteen billon dollars would provide everyone in the world with a basic diet.[1] That obscure fact reveals much about the world we live in. Many are in desperate need, with 1 in 7 of the world's population going hungry every day. But such suffering is largely hidden from those of us who live in affluent countries like Britain. Some, of course, have slipped through the benefit net and are reduced to begging to survive, but the majority of people in our country are enjoying a period of unprecedented prosperity. That is the world we live in as Christians in the West; an affluent society that is marked by two powerful forces: materialism and consumerism.

Materialism and consumerism

Materialists think that observable things are the only reality. They think this world is all there is, and live on the basis of that assumption. Materialism leads automatically to consumerism.

Details of an eighteen-month spending-spree by Elton John recently emerged in a court case. Between January 1996 and July 1997 he spent an average of £2 million a month. Purchases included four Bentley Azures, £293,000-worth of flowers and a wig, for his fiftieth birthday party, which cost £3,500. He said at the time, 'I love my possessions. I get more love from them than from most human beings.'[2]

Most of us do not have the resources to compete with Elton John, but in our more modest way we are often driven by consumerism. We buy things we do not need because they give us an identity, an image we present to the world. So the clothes we wear, the CDs we listen to, the cars we drive and the houses we live in are all statements of how we want to be seen by others. The advertising industry drives this consumerism. Its tactics are blatant, and yet we still believe the lie. We fool ourselves that if we consume that drink, we will be the life and soul of the party, and if we use that shampoo, we will be irresistible – so we spend, spend, spend.

Christians are certainly not immune to the pressures of materialism and consumerism, and we are often unaware of their influence on us. A friend of mine asked an eminent Christian leader what he thought was the greatest snare for Christians in the West. He replied, 'Materialism. If you get bitten by that drug, you may well stay a Christian but you'll be a very small Christian. Consumerism chokes the life out of many, many Christians.'

It is vital that we understand God's perspective on money and possessions if we are to prevent ourselves from being conformed into the world's mould. There is a great deal of teaching on the subject in the Bible. All we can do in this brief survey is to get a sense of the major themes as they are presented through Scripture.

1. The pattern of the kingdom – money and possessions are good gifts from God

Some religions see God as entirely separate from the material realm and concerned only with the spiritual realm. As a result, God has little or nothing to say about how we should regard and use our money and possessions. But we cannot think like that when we remember how the Bible starts: 'In the beginning God created the heavens and the earth' (Genesis 1:1). He is the Creator and owner of all things, spiritual and material. 'The earth is the LORD's and everything in it' (Psalm 24:1). As a result, we should be both grateful and good stewards.

We should be grateful
Paul writes, ' . . . everything God created is good, and nothing is to be rejected if it is received with thanksgiving . . . ' (1 Timothy 4:4). In the context of 1 Timothy, Paul is opposing some ascetics who denied themselves good pleasures, such as marriage and certain foods, and told others that they should not enjoy them either. But Paul insists that they are good gifts of a loving Creator, which he wants us to enjoy. God wants us to take pleasure in what he gives us.

The Bible does call us to give sacrificially, but that does not mean that we should keep nothing but the bare necessities for ourselves. Some Christians feel guilty whenever they spend money. They can never have a meal in a restaurant with friends or buy a decent piece of furniture because they think of all the other ways the money could have been spent. They need to remember that God is the loving Creator who wants them to enjoy the good gifts he has provided for them. But that does not give us an excuse to be selfish gluttons who use all that we have for our own pleasure and enjoyment. If God is the ultimate owner of everything, then we are merely stewards.

We should be good stewards
Our house, computer, money and all we own belong to God and

not us. If we understood that truth, it would revolutionize the way we use our possessions and view our giving. Someone has said we should consider not how much of our money we will give to God's work but how much of God's money we will keep for ourselves. One day we will have to stand before him and give an account of how we have used what he has entrusted to us (Luke 16:1–2).

2. The perished kingdom – money and possessions can be spiritually dangerous

Money and possessions are good gifts of God's creation but, now that sin has entered the world, they can be spiritually dangerous. They can be tools the devil uses to lead us into sin.

Idolatry

Jesus told one young man, 'Go, sell everything you have and give to the poor, and you will have treasure in heaven' (Mark 10:21). But the young man was rich and, faced with a choice between his wealth and following Christ, he chose the former. Jesus does not give a general command to each of his followers to forsake possessions, but he does say to all of us, 'No-one can serve two masters. Either he will hate the one and love the other, or he will be devoted to the one and despise the other. You cannot serve both God and Money' (Matthew 6:24). We have to decide which will come first.

The comedian Jack Benny had a reputation as a miser. He liked to tell the story, no doubt invented, of a time when he was accosted by an armed robber with the words, 'Your money or your life.' After a long pause, the robber said, 'Well?' 'Don't rush me, I'm thinking about it,' replied Benny.[3]

Many people today live as if their possessions are their life. A car bumper-sticker summed up the attitude: 'He who dies with the most toys wins.' But such attitudes are idolatrous. There is only one God and we should live for him and not for anything in this world.

I have seen many keen young Christians lose their spiritual

fervour as they get older. Often it is because they begin to worship money and possessions. Their priorities gradually shift as their salary and mortgage increase, until Christ is relegated to second place in their lives, or even lower. We need to be on our guard against the idolatry of materialism.

Do not covet

The Bible never says, 'Money is the root of all evil.' As we have seen, money in itself is a good gift of God's creation and, even if it can lead to sin, there are plenty of other roots to evil. But Paul does write that 'the *love* of money is *a* root of all kinds of evil' (1 Timothy 6:10, my emphasis). He urges us to be content with what we have and not long for more.

Coveting has become a national obsession. Thirty million Britons play the Lotto each week, spending an average of £3.34 per person.[4] But plenty of people who never buy a lottery ticket still covet. A Christian who is relatively poor can allow bitterness and jealousy to creep in. She begins to feel resentful of the big houses, smart cars and expensive holidays enjoyed by others in the church. Instead of praising God for what she has, she complains about what she does not have. Another believer is comparatively rich, but he is never satisfied. Within days of settling into his first home he is dreaming of the next, with more bedrooms, a bigger garden and in a smarter area. He always wants more. Such discontentment can have devastating spiritual effects. It can lead to greed, jealousy, dishonesty and ingratitude and, in the end, it can lead away from Christ: 'Some people, eager for money, have wandered from the faith and pierced themselves with many griefs' (1 Timothy 6:10).

Do not hoard

Now listen, you rich people, weep and wail because of the misery that is coming upon you. Your wealth has rotted, and moths have eaten your clothes. Your gold and silver are

corroded. Their corrosion will testify against you and eat
your flesh like fire. You have hoarded wealth in the last days.
Look! The wages you failed to pay the workmen who
mowed your fields are crying out against you. The cries of
the harvesters have reached the ears of the Lord Almighty.
You have lived on earth in luxury and self-indulgence.
(James 5:1–5)

Those words were read to a group of American ministers a few
years ago. They clearly did not know their Bibles very well and
were indignant. Their conclusion was that the writer was a
dangerous anarchist who should be deported from the country.[5]
James certainly uses very strong language. He is not condemning
the rich simply because they are wealthy. There is nothing wrong
with having wealth; everything depends on how we use it. James
is provoked by the fact that these rich people have accumulated
far more than they could ever use themselves, but instead of using
the surplus for the good of others, they have let it rot.

Perhaps we should do an inventory of our possessions. Many
are, no doubt, put to good use. But what about all those old
coats in the cupboard that have not been worn for years? Or the
expensive necklace that is no longer fashionable, so it stays in
the deposit box in the bank? Or all those old books and CDs that
haven't been touched for ages? Could they be put to better use if
given to someone, or sold and the money used profitably? What
about our savings? Of course, it is right that we save, so that we can
make provision for ourselves and our families, not just for now but
in the future as well. But there comes a time when prudent saving,
which is right and good, becomes selfish hoarding.

3. The promised kingdom – a promise of material blessing

God tells Abraham, 'To your offspring I will give this land'
(Genesis 12:7). The blessings God promises will, at least partly, be

material. God is not just concerned with our spirits. His promises encompass the whole of life.

4. The partial kingdom – justice and prosperity in the land

God fulfils his promise to Abraham and brings the people of Israel into the Promised Land. The land is then divided so that every family receives a share in its blessings. But they are not free to use their property entirely as they wish. The land is God's gift and they are responsible to him as his stewards for how they use it.

God's concern for justice

God's law was intended to ensure justice and fair distribution of the material blessings in the land. There is a concern to help the needy and to prevent an increasing gap between rich and poor. The land was to lie fallow in the Sabbath year. That law is motivated not just by ecological concerns but also by humanitarian ones: ' . . . during the seventh year let the land lie unploughed and unused. Then the poor among your people may get food from it' (Exodus 23:11). Legislation also requires that debts should be cancelled every seven years and Hebrew slaves freed (Exodus 21:1–11; Deuteronomy 15:1–18). That concern to prevent permanent large differentials between rich and poor is also reflected in the Jubilee year (Leviticus 25:8–55). The law requires that every fifty years all land should be returned to the family who originally owned it. The poor are also cared for through tithes that require Israelites to set aside a tenth of their produce. This is to provide not only for the Levites who serve in the tabernacle and have no land of their own, but for the aliens, fatherless and widows as well (Deuteronomy 14:28–29).

How should we regard these Old Testament laws? The New Testament never commands us to obey them to the letter or to put pressure on our governments to enact them. They were

---

- Usury is the charging of interest on a loan, a practice that was expressly forbidden to the Israelites: 'If you lend money to one of my people among you who is needy, do not be like a money-lender; charge him no interest' (Exodus 22:25).

- This practice was also forbidden to Christians by the Third Lateran Council (1179). That strict prohibition has now been removed and is rightly seen as unnecessary. The law against usury was introduced at a time when loans were not commercial (to help establish or extend a business), but were almost exclusively charitable (to help someone in need). The central concern was the well-being of the poor.

- The New Testament never repeats the prohibition. Christians are free to give and receive loans at interest. The principle of protecting the well-being of the poor must still apply. Loan sharks who take advantage of others' financial distress to charge excess interest, and rich governments and banks who do the same with poor nations, are rightly condemned.

Figure 18. Usury

designed to be implemented at a time when the people of God were a nation living in his land. We live in very different days since the coming of Christ. But, even if the specifics of these laws are not binding on us, the principles behind them certainly are. We should care for the poor and needy ourselves and also, in so far as we can, influence our governments to have the same concern both within the nation and throughout the world.

Is prosperity a reward for obedience?

God presents two possibilities to the Israelites as they are about to enter the land. If they disobey, they will be cursed and ultimately evicted from the land. But if they obey, they will be blessed. That blessing is described in material terms: 'The LORD will grant you abundant prosperity – in the fruit of your womb, the young of your livestock and the crops of your ground – in the land he swore to your forefathers to give you' (Deuteronomy 28:11). There is similar language in the book of Proverbs:

> Misfortune pursues the sinner,
>> but prosperity is the reward of the righteous.
>
> (13:21)

When blessing does come to the Israelites it is described in very material terms, in particular at the high point of the kingdom under Solomon (e.g. 1 Kings 4:20–28). Such passages are quoted by the proponents of the 'prosperity gospel', who teach that God will ensure that we prosper materially if we are obedient to Christ. How should we respond to this teaching?

A basic principle of biblical interpretation is that we should take careful note of both the literary and biblical context of a text.

Literary context

We should be aware of the type of literature we are reading. For example, we do not take Robert Burns' words, 'My love is like a red, red rose', literally. They are poetic. When we read the book of Proverbs we should recognize that we are not being given absolute statements that always apply. Proverbs are pithy statements that encapsulate general principles. We say, 'Practice makes perfect'; but no-one believes that is always literally true. I could practise painting for years and still be hopeless. We misread Proverbs 13:21 if we understand it to say that the godly will always be wealthy.

Biblical context

All Scripture is from God and cannot contradict itself, so we must take into account the whole of the Bible's teaching on a subject to see how it fits together. Even in the Old Testament the general principle that the godly are prosperous is challenged, for example, in the story of Job and in Psalm 73.

We also need to be aware of where we are in the Bible's unfolding story-line. The fulfilment of God's covenant promises to Abraham was significantly tied to this world in the Old Testament. Blessing from God came largely from peace and prosperity in the land. But the New Testament makes it clear that that fulfilment is only partial. What the Israelites enjoyed in the land was a shadow of the substance we can receive in Christ. Whereas they received material prosperity in a physical place, we praise God, 'who has blessed us in the heavenly realms with every spiritual blessing in Christ' (Ephesians 1:3).

Christians are not promised material prosperity in this world. When some believers were imprisoned for their faith and had their property confiscated, the writer to the Hebrews did not tell them that if they obeyed God he would release them and return their possessions. He rather reminded them that they had 'better and lasting possessions' (Hebrews 10:33–34). There will be an important physical element to the ultimate fulfilment of God's promises, but it will be in the new heavens and new earth when his people will enjoy prosperity in every sense for ever.

5. The prophesied kingdom – God's concern for justice

God is concerned not just with the religious life of the Israelites, but also with their greed and injustice. Through the prophets he gives frequent condemnations of their disobedience of his command to care for the poor:

> You trample on the poor
> and force him to give you grain.
> Therefore, though you have built stone mansions,
> you will not live in them;
> though you have planted lush vineyards,
> you will not drink their wine.
> (Amos 5:11)

'I will come near to you for judgment. I will be quick to
testify against ... those who defraud labourers of their wages,
who oppress the widows and the fatherless, and deprive
aliens of justice, but do not fear me.'
(Malachi 3:5)

An advert appeared in a newspaper, headed: 'Unpleasant
manager required'. It continued:

'We are a high-pressure company and we work for money.
We push ourselves hard and we will push you hard. We are
not looking for management to hold our hands. We want
nasty, not nice. If you are the kind of person who can make
things happen, we want to hear from you. Wimps need not
apply.'

At least they were honest. Compassion and justice are not
qualities that are admired in that kind of hard-nosed world. The
law of love is ignored; it is supply-and-demand that counts.
'Charge as much as you can get and if that forces the small family
firm out of business, so be it.' Profit counts more than people. Mrs
Jones may have worked faithfully in accounts for thirty years, but
she has never really got on top of the computer system and is not
as quick as she used to be, so it is time she went. A younger
employee will offer better value for money. That country estate
may be making huge profits, but still the manager decides not to
renew the leases of some who have lived there for years. He can
make far more money if he rents the cottages on the open market.
If the tenants have to leave the area and go miles away from their
families to find a house they can afford to buy, that is not his
problem.

Many of us in the course of our work face difficult decisions
that affect others. Sometimes in this fallen world we may be
forced to make a decision between the lesser of two evils. But we
all need to remember that ultimately we are not accountable to

our employers or the shareholders; we are accountable to God, who is more concerned about justice than about profit margins. The market does not rule; God does. His Word calls us to submit to his authority, not just in church, but in the office, in the boardroom and in the market-place.

6. The present kingdom – money and possessions will not last

Is poverty a spiritual advantage?

Luke records that Jesus' public ministry begins when he stands up in the synagogue in Nazareth and reads from the prophet Isaiah:

> 'The Spirit of the Lord is on me,
>   because he has anointed me
>   to preach good news to the poor.
> He has sent me to proclaim freedom for
>   the prisoners
>   and recovery of sight for the blind,
> to release the oppressed,
>   to proclaim the year of the Lord's favour.'
> (Luke 4:18–19)

He then continues: 'Today this scripture is fulfilled in your hearing' (4:21). It is a staggering claim to make. He is the promised Messiah who has come to spread good news to the poor. Soon afterwards he says, 'Blessed are you who are poor, for yours is the kingdom of God' (Luke 6:20). Some conclude from these verses that poverty is a spiritual advantage. Jesus came for the poor and, whenever their cause is promoted through political change or social action, the kingdom of God advances. But the wider context of Luke's Gospel suggests that we misread these verses if we take them only in a literal way.

Jesus did give sight to the blind, but there is no record of his freeing prisoners from jail. He certainly had compassion on the poor, such as Bartimaeus the beggar, but he also saved rich tax-collectors such as Levi and Zacchaeus. He was concerned about justice on earth, but that was not the chief aim of his mission. Above all, he wanted to rescue people, both rich and poor, from their sins so that they could be restored to a right relationship with his Father. That is the focus of Luke's two volumes as he describes how Jesus fulfils his manifesto pledges at Nazareth. It was also the focus of Paul's ministry that dominates the second half of Acts. At his trial before Agrippa, Paul records some words Jesus said to him at his conversion. They have clear echoes of Isaiah 61: 'I am sending you to them [the Gentiles] to open their eyes and turn them from darkness to light, and from the power of Satan to God, so that they may receive forgiveness of sins and a place among those who are sanctified by faith in me' (Acts 26:17–18). There is freedom for the oppressed and sight for the blind, but both are understood spiritually. We should understand the 'poor' in Luke 4:18 and 6:20 in the same way.

The 'poor' are the 'poor in spirit' (Matthew 5:3), who recognize their helplessness and need before God, like David in the Psalms: 'This poor man called and the LORD heard him' (Psalm 34:6). It may be that the materially poor are better placed to see how desperately they need God's help, whereas the rich are used to relying on their own resources; but poverty in itself does not guarantee spiritual blessing. God's kingdom advances when anyone, rich or poor, repents and believes in Christ.

'Moth and rust destroy'

'Do not store up for yourselves treasures on earth, where moth and rust destroy, and where thieves break in and steal. But store up for yourselves treasures in heaven, where moth and rust do not destroy, and where thieves do not break in and steal.'
(Matthew 6:19–20)

Things in this world do not last. Our favourite clothes have a nasty habit of wearing away and treasured ornaments are prone to getting broken. Even if we do manage to preserve them intact, we will not be able to take them with us to the next world. There are no pockets in a shroud and Pickfords Removals will not even give an estimate for a move to the hereafter.

Imagine you are in an art gallery and there you see a man taking the old masters off the wall and tucking them under his arm. You ask him, 'What are you doing?' He replies, 'I have decided to become an art collector.' 'Don't be ridiculous,' you say. 'Those pictures don't belong to you and the security guards will never let you leave with them.' That annoys him. 'Don't be a killjoy. Of course they are mine, they are under my arm and I am not troubling myself with depressing thoughts of leaving.' That man is clearly out of touch with reality. And so are we, if we invest in the here and now and devote our lives to accumulating possessions that will not last and we cannot keep.

If we are wise, we will live not for this world, but for the one to come. We will 'seek first God's kingdom' (Matthew 6:33), which has broken into the present through the death and resurrection of Christ and will one day come in all its fullness when he returns.

7. The proclaimed kingdom – we should use our resources for this world and the next

We live in the last days after God's kingdom has been inaugurated in Christ, but before it has fully come. We are citizens of heaven who are called to have our eyes focused on the new creation that Christ will establish when he returns. But, meanwhile, we must live on earth in this fallen world. These two foci of our existence are reflected in the New Testament's teaching about how we should use the resources that God has given us.

We should provide for ourselves and our families

It seems that some Christians in Thessalonica were so focused on the second coming that they no longer worked to earn their living. If Christ was about to return, what was the point of continuing with normal business on earth? Paul writes to rebuke them and establishes a principle: 'If a man will not work, he shall not eat' (2 Thessalonians 3:10). It is obviously right that those who are unable to work, because of incapacity or a lack of jobs, should be supported by others, but the general principle is that we should earn money to provide for our own needs.

We are also commanded to support our families. Paul writes, 'If anyone does not provide for his relatives, and especially for his immediate family, he has denied the faith and is worse than an unbeliever' (1 Timothy 5:8). If the state offers help through pensions or residential care, we may accept, but we should remember that the prime responsibility for the care of the sick and elderly is the family. Sadly, that responsibility is frequently neglected. Great-uncle Joe is placed in a poor-quality home miles from friends and family, just because it is cheap. Granny is persuaded to stay in her house even though it is cold and isolated, so that the inheritance is kept intact and not consumed by nursing-home fees. Believers may even try to justify such behaviour by saying it may leave more money available for Christian giving. But the Lord Jesus had strong words for the Pharisees who tried to evade their responsibility to their parents in a similar way (Mark 7:9–13). Supporting our families is a prime responsibility for Christians, not a secondary one.

But what does 'support' mean? What standard of living should we aspire to for ourselves and our families? Should Christians simply cover the bare necessities and give the rest away or is it justifiable to aim higher than that? Should we make do with a terraced house, caravan holidays, a clapped-out old car and state education for the children; or can we justify a detached cottage, exotic holidays, a brand new sports car and private-school education? There is no chapter in the Bible that gives us detailed instructions about exactly how we should spend our money. It simply gives us principles and then leaves us with the responsibility of applying them. In doing so we should resist the temptation to judge others; we are each accountable to God.

I will limit myself to one of the Bible's principles: sufficiency. It is well expressed by Agur in Proverbs:

> '. . . give me neither poverty nor riches,
>   but give me only my daily bread.
> Otherwise I may have too much and disown you
>   and say "Who is the LORD?"
> Or I may become poor and steal,
>   and so dishonour the name of my God.'
> (30:8–9)

His chief concern is godliness and, for that reason, he is nervous of the extremes of both poverty and riches. Christians in the West are far more likely to err in the direction of too much wealth than too little.

We should pay taxes

Jesus said, 'Give to Caesar what is Caesar's, and to God what is God's' (Matthew 22:21). Caesar does not have the right to demand worship, but he does have the right to levy taxes. Paul writes, 'Give everyone what you owe him: If you owe taxes, pay taxes; if revenue, then revenue' (Romans 13:7). Christians are not to be dishonest or search for loopholes, but should rather gladly pay our taxes in full.

We should provide for the needy

As we have seen already, concern for the poor is an important theme throughout the Bible. It remains a responsibility for Christians. Paul tells the Galatians, '. . . as we have opportunity, let us do good to all people, especially to those who belong to the family of believers' (Galatians 6:10). We should be concerned for all people, but above all we should care for those within the family of the church. The early Christians in Jerusalem clearly did that. Luke tells us, 'All the believers were together and had everything in common. Selling their possessions and goods, they gave to anyone as he had need' (Acts 2:44–45). He then gives us an insight into what happened: 'There were no needy persons among them. For from time to time those who owned lands or houses sold them, brought the money from the sales and put it at the apostles' feet, and it was distributed to anyone as he had need' (Acts 4:34–35).

I can think of similar instances in churches today: money given anonymously to those going through hard times, missionaries provided with cars, and families given houses to live in. But there is no doubt that it could, and should, happen more.

Jesus said,

' . . . no-one who has left home or brothers or sisters or mother or father or children or fields for me and the gospel will fail to receive a hundred times as much in this present age (homes, brothers, sisters, mothers, children and fields – and with them, persecutions) and in the age to come, eternal life.'
(Mark 10:29–30)

Those verses are much quoted by prosperity preachers, but they misinterpret them. They are surely meant to be understood corporately, not just individually. I cannot expect my personal bank balance to go up just because I give more to God's work. It is in the new community of Christ that I find a new family and it is from them that I will receive a home and fields if I am in need, because God's people are expected to share with one another.

This concern for the needy among the Christian community should not be limited to the local congregation. On hearing of an impending famine in Judea, the Christians in Antioch sent a gift to help their fellow believers there (Acts 11:28–29). Paul later organized a much bigger collection for the poor in Jerusalem (Romans 14:25–28; 1 Corinthians 16:1–4; 2 Corinthians 8 – 9). Rich Christians in the West also have a responsibility to help our brothers and sisters elsewhere in the world, many of whom live in conditions of extreme poverty.

We should support gospel work

> The elders who direct the affairs of the church well are worthy of double honour, especially those whose work is preaching and teaching. For the Scripture says, 'Do not muzzle the ox while it is treading out the grain,' and 'The worker deserves his wages.'
> (1 Timothy 5:17–18)

Paul chose not to receive financial support from Christians but to work as a tentmaker instead, to avoid the accusation that he preached only to make money. However, he insisted that he did have the right to such payment (1 Corinthians 9:3–12), and he expected churches to provide it for others. As the ox should be able to benefit from its labour, so should gospel workers. They should be freed from the necessity of earning a living by the generous giving of Christian people. That enables them to concentrate on their work without distraction.

Our prime responsibility is to provide proper support for those who serve our own churches, but we should also be concerned for the work of the gospel elsewhere. The great heroes of world mission include not just those on the front line, but also those who have worked hard so that they can give generously and thus free others to preach the gospel. It may be that your greatest contribution to the evangelization of the world could be through your money. Ten people earning an average income and giving 10% can pay for one gospel worker between them. Those on high salaries can pay for one worker, or more, on their own. So if you have the gift of making money, use it for God's kingdom and store up treasure for yourself in heaven.

Christian giving is:

- *Supernatural.* '... we want you to know about the grace that God has given the Macedonian churches' (2 Corinthians 8:1). The generous giving of the Macedonian churches was not so much something they did, as something God enabled them to do. We should pray for the gift of generosity.

- *Spontaneous.* 'Each man should give what he has decided in his heart to give, not reluctantly or under compulsion, for God loves a cheerful giver' (2 Corinthians 9:7). We should certainly plan our giving (see below). The point here is that true Christian giving flows from a grateful heart rather than external pressure.

- *Sacrificial.* '... they gave as much as they were able, and even beyond their ability' (2 Corinthians 8:3). Our model in giving is the Lord Jesus, who, 'though he was rich, yet for your sakes he became poor, so that you through his poverty might become rich' (2 Corinthians 8:9).

- *Systematic.* 'On the first day of every week, each one of you should set aside a sum of money in keeping with his income' (1 Corinthians 16:2). We should plan what we give in proportion to our income. In the Old Testament times, a 'tithe', 10%, was required, but that principle is never repeated in the New Testament. It may be a good starting point for Christians, but many, especially in the West, should no doubt give more.

- *Symbolic.* '... they gave themselves first to the Lord' (2 Corinthians 8:5). The money the Macedonians gave was symbolic of the lives they had already given to Christ. He wants not just our financial resources, but everything we have and are.

Figure 19. Christian giving

8. The perfected kingdom – true prosperity for ever

'Never again will they hunger;
    never again will they thirst.
The sun will not beat upon them,
    nor any scorching heat.
For the Lamb at the centre of the throne will be their
        shepherd;
he will lead them to springs of living water.
And God will wipe away every tear from their eyes.'
(Revelation 7:16–17)

The struggles of this life will not continue for ever. When Christ returns, he will remove all that spoils life on earth. There will be no more poverty or injustice. All his people will enjoy eternal life in a perfect new creation. The Lamb who was slain for us will be the shepherd who provides for us in every way, both materially and spiritually.

Summary

1. The pattern of the kingdom *(Genesis 1 – 2)*	Money and possessions are good gifts from God
2. The perished kingdom *(Genesis 3)*	Money and possessions can be spiritually dangerous
3. The promised kingdom *(Genesis 12)*	A promise of material blessing
4. The partial kingdom *(Exodus – 2 Chronicles)*	Justice and prosperity in the land
5. The prophesied kingdom *(Ezra – Malachi)*	God's concern for justice
6. The present kingdom *(Gospels)*	Money and possessions will not last
7. The proclaimed kingdom *(Acts – Revelation)*	We should use our resources for this world and the next
8. The perfected kingdom	True prosperity for ever

Figure 20. Wealth and possessions

Bible study

1 Timothy 6:6–19

verses 6–10
What does 'contentment' mean?

How does our society make it hard for us to be content?

How much should we be satisfied with?

In what ways does the world encourage us 'to get rich'?

Why is that so dangerous?

How can we protect ourselves against it?

verses 11–16
What should our ambitions be?

Where should we be focused?

What practical steps could we take to ensure that our goals are God's and not the world's?

verses 17–19
Who are the rich?

Are we included?

What are they commanded to do?

How can we prevent ourselves putting our 'hope in wealth'?

Where should we give our money?

How much should we give?

What is the greatest challenge God has given you from this passage in your:

• Attitudes?

• Behaviour?

The work of the Spirit is the work of salvation

It is ironic that, although it is through the Spirit that all Christians are in Christ, we manage to be more divided over our understanding of him and his work than over almost any other Christian doctrine. Part of the problem is that we often have an imbalanced view of his role. We focus on the minor details rather than on the Bible's main emphasis. I hope this brief survey of the Spirit's developing work throughout Scripture will serve to direct us back to where our focus should be. We will see that the Spirit shares the great goal of both the Father and the Son: to achieve the eternal plan of salvation. He is not operating a side-show while the Father and the Son continue with their work of calling people into the kingdom. The members of the Trinity all co-operate to accomplish the same mission; each has a vital role to play.

In this brief chapter there will not be space to address many of the debates that dominate much of our discussion about the Spirit today. You will have to look elsewhere for detailed consideration of subjects such as the place of signs and wonders in evangelism, the exact nature of spiritual gifts and the extent to which they are given today. But I hope this chapter will help to put those debates into perspective. If we can start by agreeing on the main features of the Bible's presentation of the Spirit's work, we may find that the more contested areas become a little less important and so less divisive than we had previously thought.

As we follow the Spirit's work through the Bible's plot-line, we will not see any change in his character. He is an eternal, divine being who never changes. But although he stays the same, his ministry develops as salvation history unfolds.

1. The pattern of the kingdom – the Spirit is God's agent in creation

The Spirit is first mentioned in the second verse of the Bible: 'Now the earth was formless and empty, darkness was over the surface of the deep, and the Spirit of God was hovering over the waters' (Genesis 1:2). At first it is not clear what the Spirit is doing as he hovers over the unformed universe, but the next words give us a clue; 'And God said, "Let there be light" ' (Genesis 1:3). There is a very close connection in the Bible between God's Spirit and his word. The Hebrew word for Spirit is *ruach*, which also means 'breath'. The New Testament's Greek word *pneuma* can also mean either. That is significant because breath and speech go together. Just as all Scripture is 'God-breathed' (2 Timothy 3:16), so all our words are expressed on our breath. That explains the close link in the Bible between breath, speech or 'word', and spirit. There is an example in Psalm 33:6:

By the word of the LORD were the heavens made,
  their starry host by the breath of his mouth.

In the parallelism of the Hebrew poetry, the second part of the verse is another way of saying the first: 'the word of the LORD' and 'the breath of his mouth' are the same. The Spirit (*ruach*) was God's agent in creation. That may explain why God refers to himself in the plural in Genesis 1:26: 'Let *us* make man in our image' (my emphasis).

It is not surprising to find the Spirit active before creation because he is divine and therefore eternal. That becomes clearer later in the Bible. He is a personal being who can be grieved and even lied to (Isaiah 63:10; Acts 5:3; Ephesians 4:30). When Jesus tells his disciples that he will send the Spirit to be the 'Paraclete' or 'Counsellor', he refers to him quite deliberately with the personal pronoun ('he') rather than the neuter ('it') which would more naturally have been used to agree with the neuter noun *pneuma* (John 14:26; 15:26; 16:8, 13–14). He is personal because he is God.

2. The perished kingdom – the Spirit's word is disobeyed

Adam and Eve disobey God's word, and the whole of creation, all that God made, is spoilt. Now there is more creative, restorative work to be done and the rest of the Bible describes the activity of God, Father, Son and Holy Spirit, in salvation.

3. The promised kingdom – the gift of the Spirit is promised

God promises to bless Abraham and his descendants (Genesis 12:1–3). Paul later tells the Galatians that those descendants consist of all, both Jew and Gentile, who are justified by faith in Christ. The blessing promised to Abraham is the gift of the Spirit: 'He redeemed us in order that the blessing given to Abraham might come to the Gentiles, through Christ Jesus, so that by faith we might receive the promise of the Spirit' (Galatians 3:14).

4. The partial kingdom – the mighty wind of God

God's Spirit was active during the history of Israel. The word *ruach* appears often in the Old Testament. As we have seen, it can mean 'breath' or 'spirit', and it can also mean 'wind', usually wind in motion. We have to examine the context to know whether the word refers to normal breath or wind, or if it speaks of the Spirit. When used of God, *ruach* refers to his violent, powerful energy as in Micah 3:8:

> But as for me, I am filled with power,
>   with the Spirit of the LORD.

God's Spirit in the Old Testament 'is, as it were, the blast of God – the irresistible power by which he accomplishes his purposes'.[1] Michael Green comments,

> I believe we have to take this aspect of the Spirit very
> seriously today. We have grown used to expecting the Spirit
> of God to speak in a gentle whisper, not a roaring wind.
> We have sought him in the promptings of our hearts or the
> resolutions of our committees. We are in danger of
> forgetting that it is God we are talking about: the God who
> created us, the God who sustains us and has sovereign rights
> over us.[2]

It is by his Spirit that God works to bring his promises to partial fulfilment in Israel's history.

The Spirit defeats God's enemies

Israel can truly be God's people only when they have been delivered from the rule of human oppressors. They are incapable of doing that themselves, but the Spirit empowers their leaders.

It was by the Spirit that Moses led the people out of Egypt:

Then his people recalled his days of old,
    the days of Moses and his people –
where is he who brought them through the sea,
    with the shepherd of his flock?
Where is he who set
    his Holy Spirit among them,
who sent his glorious arm of power
    to be at Moses' right hand,
who divided the waters before them,
    to gain for himself everlasting renown,
who led them through the depths?
(Isaiah 63:11–13)

It was by the Spirit that the judges delivered God's people:

But when they cried out to the LORD, he raised up
for them a deliverer, Othniel son of Kenaz, Caleb's
younger brother, who saved them. The Spirit of the
LORD came upon him, so that he became Israel's judge
and went to war. The LORD gave Cushan-Rishathaim
king of Aram into the hands of Othniel, who overpowered
him.
(Judges 3:9–10; see also 6:34; 14:6)

The Spirit establishes relationship with God

God defeats his enemies in order that his people might enjoy an
exclusive relationship with him. There are hints of that relationship in the Old Testament. It is seen especially in the way God
speaks to his people by the Spirit.

God speaks to the elders at the time of Moses:

He [Moses] brought together seventy of their elders and
made them stand round the Tent. Then the LORD came
down in the cloud and spoke with him, and he took of the
Spirit that was on him and put the Spirit on the seventy

elders. When the Spirit rested on them, they prophesied, but they did not do so again.
(Numbers 11:24–25)

God speaks to David:

'The Spirit of the LORD spoke through me;
   his word was on my tongue.'
(2 Samuel 23:2)

The Israelites do enjoy a real relationship with God by the Holy Spirit, but it is incomplete. That explains the prayer of Moses in Numbers 11:29 after the seventy elders have prophesied: 'I wish that all the LORD's people were prophets and that the LORD would put his Spirit on them!' His wish is never fulfilled in the Old Testament. The Spirit comes on special people for special tasks, such as kings (1 Samuel 10:6; 16:13), prophets (Ezekiel 2:2), and even craftsmen (Exodus 31:3). But most Israelites never know the blessing that Moses prays for.

5. The prophesied kingdom – the Spirit-filled Messiah will come to bring salvation

It is by the Spirit that the prophets receive, proclaim and write God's Word (Ezekiel 2:2). They point to a time of fulfilment in the future when the Spirit will play a crucial role.

The Spirit will fill the Messiah
Just as the great leaders of the past had received the gift of the Spirit, so the perfect king, the Christ, who will come in the future, will be filled with the Spirit.

A shoot will come up from the stump of Jesse;
   from his roots a Branch will bear fruit.

The Spirit of the LORD will rest on him ...
(Isaiah 11:1–2)

'Here is my servant, whom I uphold,
   my chosen one in whom I delight;
I will put my Spirit on him ... '
(Isaiah 42:1)

The Spirit of the Sovereign LORD is on me,
   because the LORD has anointed me
   to preach good news to the poor.
(Isaiah 61:1)

The Spirit will be given to all God's people

One day Moses' prayer in Numbers 11 will be answered:

'I will give you a new heart and put a new spirit in you; I will
remove from you your heart of stone and give you a heart of
flesh. And I will put my Spirit in you and move you to follow
my decrees and be careful to keep my laws.'
(Ezekiel 36:26–27)

'And afterwards,
   I will pour out my Spirit on all people.
Your sons and daughters will prophesy,
   your old men will dream dreams,
   your young men will see visions.
Even on my servants, both men and women,
   I will pour out my Spirit in those days.'
(Joel 2:28–29)

The Spirit will be agent of a new creation

God's ultimate goal is not just to save a people, but to put
everything right so they have a perfect place to live in. The
coming of God's Christ will make that possible and the Spirit

will be poured out. Isaiah proclaims that the world will remain a wasteland 'till the Spirit is poured upon us from on high, and the desert becomes a fertile field, and the fertile field a forest' (Isaiah 32:14–15). The result will be a new world that is perfectly restored.

6. The present kingdom – Jesus is the Spirit-filled Messiah

The Holy Spirit is mentioned seven times in the first two chapters of Luke's Gospel. It is by the Spirit that he is conceived, develops, is led into the wilderness to be tempted and exercises his ministry (Luke 1:35, 80; 4:1, 14). Luke is telling us plainly that the age of the Spirit has come. Various witnesses confirm that Jesus is the Spirit-filled Messiah promised by the prophets.

John the Baptist
Crowds go into the Judean wilderness to be baptised by John, but he points away from himself to the one who is to come and says, 'I baptise you with water. But one more powerful than I will come, the thongs of whose sandals I am not worthy to untie. He will baptise you with the Holy Spirit and with fire' (Luke 3:16). It will be through Jesus that the prophecies about the Spirit coming on all God's people will be fulfilled.

God the Father
Jesus identifies with sinful humanity to such an extent that he is even willing to submit to John's baptism. At that moment heaven opens. Luke tells us that 'the Holy Spirit descended on him in bodily form like a dove. And a voice came from heaven: "You are my Son, whom I love; with you I am well pleased"' (Luke 3:22). God is fulfilling what he has said through the prophet Isaiah: 'I will put my Spirit on him' (Isaiah 42:1).

The Lord Jesus himself

Jesus begins his public ministry by identifying himself as the one of whom Isaiah spoke:

> 'The Spirit of the Lord is on me,
>   because he has anointed me
>   to preach good news to the poor.'
> (Luke 4:18)

His actions confirm that he is indeed the one he claims to be. It is by the Spirit that he performs great miracles, thus showing his superiority over Satan and his ability to introduce the new creation. After he has healed a demon-possessed man, the Pharisees say, 'It is only by Beelzebub, the prince of demons, that this fellow drives out demons.' Jesus points out how illogical that would be: 'If Satan drives out Satan, he is divided against himself. How then can his kingdom stand? . . . But if I drive out demons by the Spirit of God, then the kingdom of God has come upon you' (Matthew 12:26–28).

A gift for the future

The activity of God's Spirit through God's King clearly points to the fact that God's kingdom has come. But all God's promises have not yet been fulfilled. The apostle John explains why in his Gospel. He quotes Jesus' words: 'Whoever believes in me, as the Scripture has said, streams of living water will flow from within him', and then comments, 'By this he meant the Spirit, whom those who believed in him were later to receive. Up to that time the Spirit had not been given, since Jesus had not yet been glorified' (John 7:38–39).

Jesus is glorified in his crucifixion, resurrection and ascension. The miracles are skirmishes in Jesus' war with Satan that reveal his authority over him, but the decisive battle takes place on the cross. Only once Jesus has suffered in the place of sinners, and Satan's sting has thus been drawn, is he able to pour out his Spirit on people and begin to introduce the new creation.

John's account of Jesus' breathing on the disciples and saying,

'Receive the Holy Spirit' (John 20:21) does not clash with this timetable. This event should not be understood as John's equivalent of the day of Pentecost, the moment when the Spirit is given to all God's people. Not only would he be contradicting Luke, who tells us that the Spirit was given after the ascension, but he would also be contradicting himself. He is quite clear that Christ must first be exalted before the Spirit comes (John 7:39; 14:16–17; 16:7). We should understand this endowment of the Spirit to the disciples as a particular gift for a particular task, namely their new ministry of forgiving sins (John 20:23). The gift of the Spirit to the whole church is still to come.

7. The proclaimed kingdom – the Spirit is given to all God's people

Luke's Gospel ends with the risen Jesus speaking to his disciples and telling them what is about to take place. They are to be his witnesses to all the world, but they must not start that task until they have received the gift of the Spirit: 'I am going to send you what my Father has promised; but stay in the city until you have been clothed with power from on high' (Luke 24:49). The same instruction and promise are given at the start of Acts, just before Jesus ascends to heaven:

> 'Do not leave Jerusalem, but wait for the gift my Father promised, which you have heard me speak about. For John baptised with water, but in a few days you will be baptised with the Holy Spirit ... You will receive power when the Holy Spirit comes on you; and you will be my witnesses.'
> (Acts 1:4–5, 8)

The disciples do not have to wait long. All the believers were in one place when they 'were filled with the Holy Spirit' (Acts 2:4). Peter explains the strange events by quoting Scripture:

This is what was spoken by the prophet Joel:
> 'In the last days, God says,
>> I will pour out my Spirit on all people ...
>> I will pour out my Spirit in those days,
>> and they will prophesy.'

(Acts 2:16–18)

Moses' prayer in Numbers 11:29 has at last been answered.

The Spirit and Christ

The New Testament makes it clear that the Spirit is not inaugurating a new work of God. He is continuing the work of Christ by applying it to people's lives so they can benefit from it. Jesus himself speaks of this very close relationship between his and the Spirit's work in his last discourse to the disciples as recorded in John 14 – 16.

The Spirit replaces Jesus

> 'I will ask the Father, and he will give you another
> Counsellor to be with you for ever – the Spirit of truth. The
> world cannot accept him, because it neither sees him nor
> knows him. But you know him, for he lives with you and
> will be in you. I will not leave you as orphans; I will come
> to you.'

(John 14:16–18)

Jesus has warned his disciples that he is about to leave them, but he comforts them by promising to send them a new helper. Some translations use the word *paraclete* instead of 'counsellor', staying close to the Greek word. It is a compound word taken from *para* (alongside) and *klētos* (called). That gives us an idea of what Jesus is promising: 'someone who is called alongside'. The word was used in the first century of a friend who would go with you to court to offer support. No single English word quite captures the meaning. Different translations have spoken of the 'helper', 'advocate' or 'strengthener'.

It is important to know that Jesus speaks of *another* counsellor. He has been the counsellor to the disciples while he has been with them on earth, but now that he is leaving, he promises to ensure that they are not left without the help they need. He will send the Holy Spirit to take his place. But notice the language he uses. He tells them, 'I will not leave you as orphans; *I* will come to you' (v. 18, my emphasis). The work of the Spirit is so closely bound to the work of Jesus that we could almost say that the Spirit is 'Jesus' other self'. The New Testament refers to him as 'the Spirit of Jesus' (Acts 16:7) and 'the Spirit of Christ' (Romans 8:9).

The Spirit points to Jesus

'All this I have spoken while still with you. But the Counsellor, the Holy Spirit, whom the Father will send in my name, will teach you all things and will remind you of everything I have said to you.'
(John 14:25–26)

'I have much more to say to you, more than you can now bear. But when he, the Spirit of truth, comes, he will guide you into all truth. He will not speak on his own; he will speak only what he hears, and he will tell you what is yet to come. He will bring glory to me by taking from what is mine and making it known to you.'
(John 16:12–14)

These words of Jesus are a specific promise to the apostles, not to all Christians. It is their responsibility to lay the foundations of the church by passing on to others what Christ has taught them. The Spirit will ensure that they are reliable witnesses who correctly report his message.

The Spirit will not simply remind the apostles of what Jesus has said to them in the past; he will also teach them new truth that they would not have been able to understand before he had been glorified. Jesus teaches in John 16:12–14 that the revelation the Spirit gives them will come from him and its purpose will be to glorify him. That promise is fulfilled in the writing of the New Testament.

The Spirit's ministry has been likened to the job of a flood-light.[3] If we watch a football match at night, we do not spend our time looking up at the lights. Their purpose is to enable us to see the action on the field. In the same way, the Spirit does not seek to draw attention to himself; his purpose is to point us to Christ, so, if we want to honour the Spirit, we must focus on Christ.

The connection between the ministry of Jesus and the Spirit is very clear in the Bible and we must not separate what God has joined together. Jim Packer writes, 'The Spirit, we might say, is the match maker, the celestial marriage broker, whose role is to bring us and Christ together and ensure that we stay together.'[4] In the rest of this chapter we shall consider the different aspects of that great work.

The Spirit and conversion

Christ has done everything necessary for anyone who trusts him to be fully accepted by God and guaranteed a place in heaven. But no sinful human being will ever repent and believe in Christ without outside help. Each of us by nature has 'a sinful mind' that is 'hostile to God. It does not submit to God's law, nor can it do so' (Romans 8:7). We are spiritually blind, enslaved by sin and dead to God (2 Corinthians 4:4; John 8:34; Ephesians 2:1). Only by a miracle can we see, be set free and come alive spiritually. Miracles like these are some of the great works of the Spirit in our lives.

The Spirit convicts

'When he [the Holy Spirit] comes, he will convict the world of guilt in regard to sin and righteousness and judgment: in regard to sin, because men do not believe in me; in regard to

> righteousness, because I am going to the Father, where you
> can see me no longer; and in regard to judgment, because the
> prince of this world now stands condemned.'
> (John 16:8–11)

A friend of mine was once in court charged with dangerous driving. He was convinced he was innocent until a prosecution witness described what he had seen. His testimony made my friend decide to change his plea to guilty. The Holy Spirit has been sent by Jesus to achieve a similar change of heart in our lives.

We assume that it is other people who are the sinners, but the Spirit will convict us of the terrible sin of not believing in Christ. We think that, if there is a God, he must be satisfied with our lives, but the Spirit will enable us to see how low our standards are and instead recognize true righteousness in Christ. We laugh at any thought of a future judgment, but the Spirit will enable us to see its inevitability now that Satan has already been defeated at the cross.

The Spirit enlightens

> This is what we speak, not in words taught us by human
> wisdom but in words taught by the Spirit, expressing spiritual
> truths in spiritual words. The man without the Spirit does
> not accept the things which come from the Spirit of God, for
> they are foolishness to him and he cannot understand them,
> because they are spiritually discerned.
> (1 Corinthians 2:13–14)

Recently at a meal I sat next to a university professor. When he learnt I was a clergyman he asked me, 'Do you believe in God?' I was a little surprised that he felt he needed to ask that question, but I told him that I did. As we continued to talk, it soon became clear that he was baffled as to how I could believe such nonsense as the Christian message. It was 'foolishness' to him. His great intellect did not help him to understand the gospel. It is only by the Spirit that we will see God's truth.

First, we are dependent on the Spirit for the revelation he gave to the apostles in the first century, which is now preserved in the New Testament. They received words 'taught by the Spirit'. But we also depend on the Spirit to illumine the words he inspired all those years ago, so that we are able to understand and believe them today. We need him to do the same work that he did in the Thessalonians when the gospel was preached to them. Paul later told them, 'For we know, brothers loved by God, that he has

---

The work of the Spirit is very closely related to God's Word.

The Spirit inspired the Word

'All Scripture is God-breathed' (2 Timothy 3:16). The Holy Spirit ensured that the writers of the Bible wrote exactly what he wanted them to write. For example: 2 Samuel 23:2; Isaiah 59:21 (Old Testament) and John 14:25–26; 16:12–15 (New Testament).

The Spirit equips us to proclaim the Word

' . . . you will receive power when the Holy Spirit comes on you; and you will be my witnesses . . .' (Acts 1:8). The Holy Spirit enables weak people like us to present God's message in the Bible clearly and powerfully (e.g. Acts 4:8, 31).

The Spirit illuminates the Word

' . . . our gospel came to you not simply with words, but also with power, with the Holy Spirit and with deep conviction' (1 Thessalonians 1:5). The same Spirit who inspired God's Word in the first place, and then empowers Christians to proclaim it, also opens the eyes of unbelievers to understand it. It is chiefly through the Word that the Spirit convicts, regenerates and assures believers. The Word of God is 'the sword of the Spirit' (Ephesians 6:17). It follows that, if we want to honour the Spirit, we must pay careful attention to the Bible.

Figure 21. The Spirit and the Word of God

chosen you, because our gospel came to you not simply with words, but also with power, with the Holy Spirit and with deep conviction' (1 Thessalonians 1:4–5)

The Spirit regenerates

'The Spirit gives life; the flesh counts for nothing. The words I have spoken to you are spirit and they are life' (John 6:63).

Just as the Spirit was the agent of the first creation, so he is the agent of the new creation; he brings new life. Jesus' words to Nicodemus apply to all of us as those who are spiritually dead by nature: 'You must be born again' (John 3:7). The Spirit achieves that work of regeneration through the words of Jesus. Once again, we see a very close connection between word and Spirit. Peter reminds his readers, '. . . you have been born again, not of perishable seed, but of imperishable, through the living and enduring word of God' (1 Peter 1:23). Every time an individual believes the gospel and turns to Christ, a spiritual resurrection occurs; someone who was dead is now alive.

The Spirit indwells

'But you know him, for he lives with you and will be in you' (John 14:17).

The mark of those who are born again is the presence of the Holy Spirit in their lives. It is by the Spirit that we are united to Christ and thus receive all the blessings that he achieved for us through his life, death, resurrection and ascension. We become 'new creations'; 'the old has gone, the new has come!' (2 Corinthians 5:17).

This is the chief role of the Spirit. We can have no spiritual life unless we are united to Christ; and we cannot be united to Christ unless the Spirit indwells us. That explains how Paul can say, '. . . if anyone does not have the Spirit of Christ, he does not belong to Christ' (Romans 8:9).

The New Testament knows nothing of 'unspiritual Christians'. That is a contradiction in terms. It is the equivalent of referring to an 'unregenerate Christian'. If we have Christ, we have the Spirit; we could not be joined to him otherwise. We should never use language that implies that only some Christians are really spiritual and that others have not yet fully received the Spirit. That seems to have been what some Christians in Corinth were saying, but Paul stresses, 'We were all baptised by one Spirit into one body – whether Jews or Greeks, slave or free – and we were all given the one Spirit to drink' (1 Corinthians 12:13). All Christians are baptised in the Spirit at conversion when the Spirit enters their lives and joins them to Christ. 'The gift of the Holy Spirit is a *universal* Christian experience because it is an *initial* Christian experience.'[5]

The Spirit transforms

In uniting us to Christ, the great goal of the Spirit is to transform us into his likeness (Romans 8:29; 2 Corinthians 3:18).

The Spirit gives us *new desires*: 'Those who live according to the sinful nature have their minds set on what that nature desires; but those who live in accordance with the Spirit have their minds set on what the Spirit desires' (Romans 8:5).

We are born with sinful desires that focus on ourselves and away from God. But the Spirit has given us a new nature. Those who are born again find they have a new hatred of sin and a new longing to be like Jesus. How could it be otherwise now that the Holy Spirit lives within them?

The Spirit gives us *new power*: 'if you live according to the sinful nature, you will die; but if by the Spirit you put to death the misdeeds of the body, you will live' (Romans 8:13).

Our new nature does not mean the end of sin. We still live in a fallen world that tries to conform us to its ways. We still experience the strong pull of the flesh or 'sinful nature' within us. A battle rages in our hearts: 'For the sinful nature desires what is contrary to the Spirit, and the Spirit what is contrary to the sinful nature. They are in conflict with each other, so that you do not do what you want' (Galatians 5:17). Christians are still sinners, but we are never happy sinners. When we sin we do not do what we want. Paul speaks for us all when he says: 'I do not understand what I do. For what I want to do I do not do, but what I hate I do' (Romans 7:15). But we need not despair. God has not left us to struggle against sin on our own. As we battle against temptation, we can look to the Spirit to help us. It is with his power that we can begin to 'put to death the misdeeds of the body'.

The Spirit *produces fruit*: 'the fruit of the Spirit is love, joy, peace, patience, kindness, goodness, faithfulness, gentleness and self-control' (Galatians 5:22–23).

As we fight against sin in our lives, we will increasingly see Christ-like qualities developing in us. They are a sign of the Spirit's work; they are his fruit.

The Spirit assures us

'The Spirit himself testifies with our spirit that we are God's children' (Romans 8:16). Paul's great words in Romans 8:15–39 have been described as 'a transcript of the Spirit's witness'.[6] He assures those he indwells that they are God's children who, despite the sufferings of the present world, can be sure they are heading for glory. 'Nothing will be able to separate us from the love of God in Christ Jesus' (Romans 8:39).

The Spirit equips

'You will receive power when the Holy Spirit comes on you; and you will be my witnesses' (Acts 1:8). The Spirit was given on the day of Pentecost to empower the church in mission. The impact was immediate. These frightened, weak individuals, who had denied Jesus a few days before, were transformed into powerful preachers who changed the world. We too should ask God to give us the strength to carry out the same task in our generation.[7]

The Spirit equips us not only for evangelism in the world but also for service in the church. 'Now to each one the manifestation of the Spirit is given for the common good' (1 Corinthians 12:7). When the Spirit unites us to Christ, he also unites us to other Christians in one body (1 Corinthians 12:13). Just as the human

Biblical Christians have different views about the extent to which we can expect to see miracles today and whether God still gives gifts such as tongues and prophecy. Any discussion of these issues should bear in mind the following points:

- *The uniqueness of the apostles.* Miracles in the Bible are found mainly in clusters at key moments in salvation history, such as the exodus, the beginning of the age of prophecy at the time of Elijah and Elisha, and the ministry of Jesus and the apostles. The miracles performed by the apostles, and those closely associated with them, marked them out as truly God's messengers at the crucial time when they were laying the foundation of the church's teaching (Hebrews 2:3–4). Paul insisted that he was a genuine apostle because he had performed 'the things that mark an apostle – signs, wonders and miracles' (2 Corinthians 12:12).

- *The sufficiency of Scripture.* Paul tells the Ephesians that the Spirit has been revealing his truth to 'God's holy apostles and prophets' in a new way. The gospel they receive forms the 'foundation' of the church (Ephesians 2:20; 3:5). That foundation has now been established (Hebrews 1:1–2). The Bible tells us all we need to know about God and how to please him (2 Timothy 3:16–17). If we want to hear God speak to us, we must turn to Scripture.

- *The sovereignty of God.* God does not simply give us the Bible and then leave us alone. He continues to be intimately involved in our lives, as individuals and churches, in every detail. He has not changed since the first century. It may be that we cannot expect him to work in exactly the same way as he did then, but he can do. He still has the power to perform miracles and to lead us in the particular ways he wants us to go. All Christians know his sovereign activity in their lives, even if they sometimes use different language to express it.

Figure 22. Can we expect all the New Testament gifts today?

body is a unity, made up of different parts with different functions, so Christ has ensured that the members of his body, the church, have different gifts.

There is a wide variety of gifts in the church. The New Testament contains a number of lists of spiritual gifts, all of which are different (Romans 12:6–8; 1 Corinthians 12:8–11, 28–30; Ephesians 4:11; 1 Peter 4:10–11). Some appear more obviously supernatural, such as 'workers of miracles and those having gifts of healing'; others seem more mundane: 'those able to help others' and 'those with gifts of administration' (1 Corinthians 12:28). A spiritual gift is any way by which God ministers his grace through one Christian to another. There is no reason to believe that other qualities, such as an ability to play music or offer hospitality, should not be regarded as spiritual gifts when they are used to edify the church, even though they are not specifically mentioned as such in the New Testament.

These gifts should be exercised in love. It is no accident that Paul's great chapter on love (1 Corinthians 13) comes in between two chapters on gifts. He is stressing the central importance of love. We should not seek gifts in order to enhance our spiritual egos; we should rather be longing for those gifts that most enable us to serve others. Paul urges us, 'Since you are eager to have spiritual gifts, try to excel in gifts that build up the church' (1 Corinthians 14:12).

The Spirit secures

'Having believed, you were marked in him with a seal, the promised Holy Spirit, who is a deposit guaranteeing our inherit-ance until the redemption of those who are God's possession – to the praise of his glory' (Ephesians 1:13–14). God's ultimate goal is to bring us into his presence in heaven. The Spirit will make sure that this great work is completed. He is the 'firstfruits' (Romans 8:23) who points us ahead to the coming harvest. He is a 'seal' that marks us out as belonging to the age to come. He is a 'deposit', God's down-payment, who guarantees that one day we will receive the full blessings of salvation.

8. The perfected kingdom – the eternal Spirit

One day the Spirit's great work of salvation will be completed and all Christ's people will join in worship around God's throne. In his vision of heaven, John sees seven lamps burning before that throne. He identifies them as 'the seven spirits of God' (Revelation 4:5). The number seven does not imply that the Spirit is plural; it represents perfection. Just as the Spirit was with the Father in creation, so he is with him in eternity.

Conclusion

Do I have the Holy Spirit?

That was a question I asked myself when I was a young Christian after a conversation with a friend. It was clear that she doubted I had received the Spirit because I lacked certain experiences and gifts. I had been converted to Christ just a year before. I knew he had died for me, that I was forgiven and that I would be with him for eternity. My life had been transformed. There was a joy I had never known before and I found I longed to go Christ's way even though I often failed. I was a Christian; there was no doubt about that. But had I received the Spirit? I decided to read through the whole New Testament to find out what it said about the Holy Spirit. There were some things I did not fully understand, and still don't, but it soon became very clear to me that the Spirit's great ministry was to apply Christ's work of salvation to his people. The more I read, the more convinced I was that I had the Spirit in my life. How else could I have come to know Christ and be changed by him?

All those who know and love Christ enjoy 'fellowship with the Spirit' (Philippians 2:1). No doubt we will differ in our opinions of aspects of the Spirit's work, but we must keep those differences in perspective by keeping our focus where the Spirit's is: on Christ.

Does the Holy Spirit have me?

Someone once said, 'If we see the Spirit as an influence, we will want more of "it". If we see him as a person, we will want him to have more of us.' It is sadly possible to 'grieve' the Spirit (Ephesians 4:30) by resisting his work in our lives. Instead, we should consciously 'keep in step with the Spirit' (Galatians 5:25).

Paul urges us to 'be filled with the Spirit' (Ephesians 5:18). He uses the present continuous tense: 'keep on being filled'. He is not speaking of a once-for-all experience, but of a way of life. The disciples were 'filled with grief' when Jesus told them that he was leaving (John 16:6); and the people were 'filled with awe' (Luke 5:26) after Jesus healed a man. To be 'filled' means to be totally captive to those emotions. In a similar way, to be 'filled with the Spirit' means to be completely captive to his power and influence. The result is very practical. The command to be filled with the Spirit in Ephesians 5:18 is followed in the original by a series of participles that show what it will mean in practice: '. . . addressing one another in psalms and hymns and spiritual songs, singing and making melody to the Lord with all your heart, giving thanks always and for everything to God the Father in the name of our Lord Jesus Christ, submitting to one another out of reverence for Christ' (Ephesians 5:19–21, English Standard Version).

We miss so much blessing in our Christian lives because we fail to realize how much God wants to give us through his Spirit. If we depend on him, and stop resisting him, we can expect peace, progress, power and joy in the midst of all the battles of this life.

Summary

1. The pattern of the kingdom (*Genesis 1 – 2*)	The Spirit is God's agent in creation
2. The perished kingdom (*Genesis 3*)	The Spirit's word is disobeyed
3. The promised kingdom (*Genesis 12*)	The gift of the Spirit is promised
4. The partial kingdom (*Exodus – 2 Chronicles*)	The mighty wind of God
5. The prophesied kingdom (*Ezra – Malachi*)	The Spirit-filled Messiah will come to bring salvation
6. The present kingdom (*Gospels*)	Jesus is the Spirit-filled Messiah
7. The proclaimed kingdom (*Acts – Revelation*)	The Spirit is given to all God's people
8. The perfected kingdom	The eternal Spirit

Figure 23. God's Spirit

☐ Bible study

The Spirit in John's Gospel

Work through the references to the Spirit in John's Gospel and write a summary statement for each:

1:32–34

3:5–7

3:34

4:23–24

6:63

7:37–39

14:16–18

14:25–26

15:26

16:5–11

16:12–15

20:22

How do these verses answer the following questions:
• Who is the Holy Spirit?

• Who sends him?

• Who does he come to?

• What does he do?

How does this study challenge:

- Our previous thinking about the Spirit?

- Our lives? (What are the practical implications of these truths?)

6 | God and the nations
What is God's plan for the world?

I once heard Dr Chris Wright, the former Principal of All Nations Christian College, say that he had been tempted to change the name of a lecture course from 'The biblical basis of mission' to 'The missiological basis of the Bible'. Mission is not just one strand within Scripture; it is its central theme. God is a missionary God and the Bible is a missionary book.

1. The pattern of the kingdom – the Creator of all peoples

It is significant that the Bible does not begin in Genesis 12 with an account of the origins of the people of Israel. The God of Israel is not simply a tribal God. As the Creator of everything, all peoples on earth owe him their allegiance. That was a staggering claim for the tiny nation of Israel to make about their God. It was a scandal in ancient times and it remains a scandal today.

We are not free to pick and choose which God we wish to serve. There is only one God, the eternal Father, Son and Holy

Spirit, who created the universe. The appeal of the psalmist should still be made today:

> Shout for joy to the LORD, all the earth.
>   Worship the LORD with gladness;
>   Come before him with joyful songs.
> Know that the LORD is God.
>   It is he who made us, and we are his;
>   we are his people, the sheep of his pasture.
> (Psalm 100:1–3)

In one of the classrooms at my school there was an old map which pre-dated the Second World War. Large sections were coloured pink, representing the British Empire. Many people seem to think that the religious map of the world also contains a variety of colours, to indicate where different gods hold sway. Africa, Europe, America and Australasia are governed by the Christian God; but Allah is in control of the Middle East, Krishna of India, and Shintoism of Japan. But the Bible will not let us think in that way. God's empire covers the whole world. He made everything and is, therefore, the only rightful ruler over everything.

2. The perished kingdom – the human race is divided from God and each other

Adam and Eve are the forebears of all people on earth. Their fall has consequences for everyone.

At first, humanity is united and speaks just one language (Genesis 11:1). But that changes after their attempt to build the tower of Babel. It is a symbol of human pride and arrogance. They say to one another: 'Come, let us build ourselves a city, with a tower that reaches to the heavens, so that we may make a name for ourselves and not be scattered over the face of the earth'

(Genesis 11:4). God realizes how dangerous sinful humanity could be if it continues to operate in unison; there would be no limit to the evil they could produce. So he scatters them over the whole earth and gives them separate languages. They are now separated from him and from one another.

3. The promised kingdom – God promises to bless the nations

God's promises are initially focused on Abraham's descendants, the Israelites, but they have a universal scope. God tells Abraham, 'all peoples on earth will be blessed through you' (Genesis 12:3). The God who created everyone is concerned to bless people from the whole world when he acts in salvation.

As the theme of salvation develops through Scripture, it becomes clear that God will use a great king as the agent of his saving work. Jacob speaks of this king at the end of his life when he blesses his son Judah. This king will not simply rule over Israel; 'the obedience of the nations is his' (Genesis 49:10).

4. The partial kingdom – some Gentiles are drawn to Israel's God

Moses delivered God's word to the Israelites in the Pentateuch, the first five books of the Bible. They were reminded of their privileges and responsibilities with regard to other nations.

Set apart

To the LORD your God belong the heavens, even the highest heavens, the earth and everything in it. Yet the LORD set his affection on your forefathers and loved them, and he

chose you, their descendants, above all the nations, as it is
today.
(Deuteronomy 10:14–15)

President Roosevelt would sometimes take his guests outside after
dinner and direct their attention to the night sky. They would
locate the lower left-hand corner of the Great Square of Pegasus
and then a small hazy blur nearby. Then he would say, 'That is
the spiral galaxy of Andromeda. It is as large as the Milky Way. It
is one of 100 million galaxies. It is over 750 million light years from
us. It contains 100 billion stars, each larger than our sun.' Then he
would pause and continue, 'Now I think we feel small enough.
Let's go to bed.'[1] God made every one of those galaxies and stars.
We human beings are just one tiny part of the universe he created
and Israel was just one of the many peoples on earth. Why should
he be interested in them? There was nothing special about them.
They were just as sinful as others, and far less outwardly
impressive than most. In fact, they were just a bunch of slaves.
And yet God set them apart from the other nations and chose to
bless them in a special way.

Called to be different

'You are to be holy to me because I, the LORD, am holy, and
I have set you apart from the nations to be my own.'
(Leviticus 20:26)

A man who had been charged with treason was brought before
Alexander the Great. When the emperor asked for the man's name
and was told that it was 'Alexander', he said, 'Either change your
name or change your behaviour.' Such a name could not be
demeaned. The Israelites' special status as God's own people also
made demands on them. They belonged to the holy God and were
therefore expected to be a holy people, standing out from the
other nations by the way they lived. God told them, 'When you

enter the land the LORD your God is giving you, do not learn to imitate the detestable ways of the nations there' (Deuteronomy 18:9).

A kingdom of priests

'You yourselves have seen what I did to Egypt, and how I
carried you on eagles' wings and brought you to myself.
Now if you obey me fully and keep my covenant, then out of
all nations you will be my treasured possession. Although the
whole earth is mine, you will be for me a kingdom of priests
and a holy nation.'
(Exodus 19:4–6)

Just as an Israelite priest was called to represent God to the nation, so Israel as a whole was called to represent him to all the other nations. They were meant to be obviously different so that the rest of the world took notice and glorified God.

Moses stressed their responsibility again as they were about to enter the land:

See, I have taught you decrees and laws as the LORD my God
commanded me, so that you may follow them in the land
you are entering to take possession of it. Observe them
carefully, for this will show your wisdom and understanding
to the nations, who will hear about all these decrees and say,
'Surely this great nation is a wise and understanding people.'
What other nation is so great as to have their gods near them
the way the LORD our God is near us whenever we pray to
him? And what other nation is so great as to have such
righteous decrees and laws as this body of laws I am setting
before you today?
(Deuteronomy 4:5–8)

In choosing one nation, God had all nations in view. His

election of Israel was a great privilege, but a great responsibility came with it. They were to be his witnesses in the world.

Israel's witness to the world

We should not think of the Israelites' task of witness to God in New Testament terms. Apart from Jonah, the reluctant missionary to the Ninevites, they are not told to take a message to other nations. 'The nation of Israel witnesses to the saving purposes of God by experiencing them and living according to them.'[2] The focus is on attraction rather than outreach, as Gentiles see what God is doing in their midst and are drawn to them.

There are a few occasions in the Old Testament when foreigners are struck by what God is doing in Israel and are attracted to them and their God as a result. This happened especially during the reign of Solomon: 'Men of all nations came to listen to Solomon's wisdom, sent by all the kings of the world, who had heard of his wisdom' (1 Kings 4:34). Perhaps the most striking example is the Queen of Sheba. She 'heard about the fame of Solomon and his relation to the name of the LORD' and came to visit him (1 Kings 10:1). She was very struck by his great wisdom and wealth and recognized that they came from God: 'Praise be to the LORD your God, who has delighted in you and placed you on

---

- *Rahab the prostitute*: 'The LORD your God is God in heaven above and on the earth below' (Joshua 2:11).
- *Ruth the Moabite*: 'Your people will be my people and your God my God' (Ruth 1:16).
- *The Queen of Sheba*: 'Praise be to the LORD your God, who has delighted in you and placed you on the throne of Israel. Because of the LORD's eternal love for Israel, he has made you king, to maintain justice and righteousness' (1 Kings 10:9).
- *Naaman the Aramite*: 'Now I know that there is no God in all the world except in Israel' (2 Kings 5:15).

Figure 24. Gentiles who trust in the God of Israel

the throne of Israel. Because of the LORD's eternal love for Israel, he has made you king, to maintain justice and righteousness' (1 Kings 10:9). She gave gifts to Solomon and he responded by giving her 'all she desired and asked for' (10:13).

5. The prophesied kingdom – the nations will see God's glory

Judgment and the nations
Although the Israelites were the focus of the prophets' message, the nations also feature prominently. God is sovereign over all nations and can use them as his instruments. Foreign powers will defeat the kingdoms of Israel and Judah, but they will not act alone. Babylon is merely God's sword (Ezekiel 21:3) by which he exercises his judgment. But the nations are not just agents of God's judgment; they will also be its recipients (Ezekiel 25 – 32). God is concerned for righteousness in all the world, not just in Israel.

Hope and the nations
We will focus on the prophet Isaiah, who, perhaps more than any other prophet, speaks of how God's salvation will encompass all nations at the end of time.

The nations will stream to Zion

In the last days

the mountain of the LORD's temple will be established
as chief among the mountains;
it will be raised above the hills,
and all nations will stream to it.

Many peoples will come and say,

'Come, let us go up to the mountain of the LORD,

to the house of the God of Jacob.
He will teach us his ways,
   so that we may walk in his paths.'
The law will go out from Zion,
   the word of the LORD from Jerusalem.
He will judge between the nations
   and will settle disputes for many peoples.
They will beat their swords into ploughshares
   and their spears into pruning hooks.
Nation will not take up sword against nation,
   nor will they train for war any more.
(Isaiah 2:3–4)

As the nations flock to God, so his word will go out to them. The result will be universal peace.

The nations rally to the Son of David

In that day the Root of Jesse will stand as a banner for the peoples; the nations will rally to him, and his place of rest will be glorious.
(Isaiah 11:10)

Jesse was David's father. His 'root' is the great king of David's line who will rule, not just Israel, but all people.

The nations put their hope in God's Servant

'Here is my servant, whom I uphold,
   my chosen one in whom I delight;
I will put my Spirit on him
   and he will bring justice to the nations ...
In faithfulness he will bring forth justice;
   he will not falter or be discouraged
till he establishes justice on earth.

In his law the islands will put their hope.'
(Isaiah 42:1, 3–4)

The Servant will establish justice throughout the whole world.

The nations receive God's salvation

'It is too small a thing for you to be my servant
   to restore the tribes of Jacob
   and bring back those of Israel I have kept.
I will also make you a light for the Gentiles,
   that you may bring my salvation to the ends of the earth.'
(Isaiah 49:6–7)

The Servant will be rejected by his own people, but he will be
worshipped by many throughout the world.

The nations will see God's glory

'And I, because of their actions and their imaginations, am
about to come and gather all nations and tongues, and they
will come and see my glory.

'I will set a sign among them, and I will send some of
those who survive to the nations ... and to the distant islands
that have not heard of my fame or seen my glory. They will
proclaim my glory among the nations. And they will bring all
your brothers, from all the nations, to my holy mountain in
Jerusalem as an offering to the LORD ... From one New
Moon to another and from one Sabbath to another, all
mankind will come and bow down before me,' says the
LORD. 'And they will go out and look upon the dead bodies
of those who rebelled against me; their worm will not die,
nor will their fire be quenched, and they will be loathsome to
all mankind.'
(Isaiah 66:18–20, 23–24)

At Babel the human race gathered together to glorify itself, and God scattered them in judgment. But one day that judgment will be reversed. The human race will be joined together to see God's glory. They will be gathered by messengers who are sent out by God to proclaim his glory throughout the world.

A youth leader told me that she asked the members of her group to write a vision statement for their lives. She was moved to tears when her fourteen-year-old daughter wrote, 'I only exist to make God famous.' That is the goal of mission. John Piper has written, 'Mission exists because worship doesn't.'[3]

Some of the psalms focus on God's king. The exalted language they use makes it clear that he is more than a mere human king. His mission will extend not just to Israel, but to all nations.

- The nations will oppose him:

  > The kings of the earth take their stand
  >> and the rulers gather together against the LORD
  > and against his Anointed One.
  > (Psalm 2:2)

- The nations will submit to him:

  > All kings will bow down to him
  >> and all nations will serve him.
  > (Psalm 72:11)

- The nations will be blessed by him:

  > All nations will be blessed through him,
  >> and they will call him blessed.
  > (Psalm 72:17)

- The nations will praise him:

  > I will perpetuate your memory through all generations;
  >> therefore the nations will praise you for ever and ever.
  > (Psalm 45:17)

Figure 25. The king and the nations

Isaiah's prophecies are brought to a close with this magnificent vision of where the world is heading. A period of mission, when God's glory is proclaimed among the nations, is followed by a final great division. Many from all peoples will worship the LORD, but those who have refused to repent will be excluded from his presence.

6. The present kingdom – the kingdom of Jesus is for all nations

The mission of Jesus

We will concentrate on Matthew's Gospel in this section. It is the most Jewish Gospel, stressing throughout that Jesus is Israel's Messiah, but it also emphasizes that Jesus' mission will extend to all nations. Matthew is the only evangelist to record the visit of the Magi from the East. As soon as Jesus is born, they travel from far away to worship him. They are symbolic representatives of the many from all nations who will follow in their footsteps and flock to Zion, the Son of David, and the glory of God as Isaiah had foretold. But Jesus does not embark on his mission to the Gentiles immediately. He begins by focusing on the people of Israel. It is only when they reject him that God's kingdom is offered to the Gentiles.

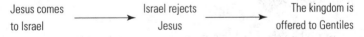

| Jesus comes to Israel | ⟶ | Israel rejects Jesus | ⟶ | The kingdom is offered to Gentiles |

Figure 26. The progression of Jesus' mission

It is clear that Jesus knew his mission would follow the pattern portrayed in Figure 26. Those three stages are reflected in the Parable of the Tenants. We will look at them in turn, starting each time with that parable and then seeing how its themes are reflected elsewhere in Jesus' teaching.

Jesus comes to Israel

> 'Listen to another parable: There was a landowner who
> planted a vineyard. He put a wall around it, dug a winepress
> in it and built a watchtower. Then he rented the vineyard to
> some farmers and went away on a journey. When the
> harvest time approached, he sent his servants to the tenants
> to collect his fruit.
>
> 'The tenants seized his servants; they beat one, killed
> another, and stoned a third. Then he sent other servants to
> them, more than the first time, and the tenants treated them
> in the same way. Last of all, he sent his son to them. "They
> will respect my son," he said.'
> (Matthew 21:33–37)

The tenants in this parable represent Israel. God gave them the
precious gift of their land, but they showed no gratitude. They
turned from him and dismissed all the prophets he sent to call
them back to himself. So God sent his own Son.

Jesus understood that he had come initially for the people of
Israel. When a Canaanite woman asked him to heal her daughter,
he replied, 'I was sent only to the lost sheep of Israel' (15:24). She
persisted and her wish was granted, but she was a rare exception
in Jesus' earthly ministry.

Israel rejects Jesus

> 'But when the tenants saw the son, they said to each other,
> "This is the heir. Come, let's kill him and take his
> inheritance." So they took him and threw him out of the
> vineyard and killed him.
>
> 'Therefore, when the owner of the vineyard comes, what
> will he do to those tenants?'
>
> 'He will bring those wretches to a wretched end . . .'
> (Matthew 21:38–41a)

There were some Jews who did accept Jesus, but the nation as a whole, represented by the religious leaders to whom he told this parable, did not. Jesus knew he would be rejected by his own people, as the prophets had foretold.

Towards the end of his earthly life, Jesus issued a solemn condemnation against the religious leaders (Matthew 23). Then, as he walked away from the temple building, he said to his disciples, 'Do you see all these things? . . . I tell you the truth, not one stone here will be left on another; every one will be thrown down' (24:2). His prophecy was fulfilled in AD 70 when the Romans destroyed the temple. God had acted in judgment against his people for their rejection of his Messiah.

The kingdom of God is offered to the Gentiles

'He will bring those wretches to a wretched end,' they replied, 'and he will rent the vineyard to other tenants, who will give him his share of the crop at harvest time.'
Jesus said to them, 'Have you never read in the Scriptures:

' "The stone the builders rejected
  has become the capstone;
the Lord has done this,
  and it is marvellous in our eyes"?

'Therefore I tell you that the kingdom of God will be taken away from you and given to a people who will produce its fruit.'
(Matthew 21:41–43)

Israel's rejection of Jesus would not deflect God's purposes. God would still make him the keystone on which the whole building of his kingdom rests. The blessings of that kingdom would then be given to the Gentiles. It is striking that Matthew's quotation of Isaiah 42:1–4, which speaks of the Servant bringing salvation to the nations, is sandwiched between two statements of Jesus' rejection by the Pharisees (Matthew 12:14, 24). Once Israel rejected Jesus, the doors of his kingdom would be opened wide to all peoples. Speaking to the centurion, on another rare occasion when a Gentile was blessed by Jesus in his earthly ministry, Jesus said, 'I say to you that many will come from the east and the west, and will take their places at the feast with Abraham, Isaac and Jacob in the kingdom of heaven. But the subjects of the kingdom will be thrown outside, into the darkness, where there will be weeping and gnashing of teeth' (Matthew 8:11–12).

The age of mission to the Gentiles will continue right up to the end of time. When the disciples asked Jesus when the end would come, he replied that there would first be wars, famines and earthquakes. And he told them, 'Then you will be handed over to be persecuted and put to death, and you will be hated by all nations because of me ... And this gospel of the kingdom will be preached in the whole world as a testimony to all nations, and then the end will come' (Matthew 24:9, 14).

The Great Commission

> Then Jesus came to them and said, 'All authority in heaven and on earth has been given to me. Therefore go and make disciples of all nations, baptising them in the name of the Father and of the Son and of the Holy Spirit, and teaching them to obey everything I have commanded you. And surely I am with you always, to the very end of the age.'
> (Matthew 28:18–20)

The crucifixion is the culmination of stage two, when Jesus is rejected. Jesus launches stage three after the resurrection when he sends his disciples to the ends of the earth. We should notice the comprehensive nature of his words.

'All authority'

As the divine Son of God, Jesus has all authority, not some. He has not shared his rule and he will not share his glory. He is the only God, not one among many. He has the right to demand the obedience of his followers in fulfilling his mission and he has the right to demand the repentance of those they address.

'All nations'

The universal Lord expects universal allegiance. His witnesses must proclaim his message in all nations: Britain and America; France and Estonia; Saudi Arabia and Azerbaijan; Somalia and the Congo; Kuwait and Japan; Chile and Peru; everywhere.

It is an astonishing command to give to a tiny band of weak disciples. The story is told of Jesus arriving in heaven after his ascension. The angel Gabriel greets him and says, 'Lord, it is wonderful that you have died and risen so that people from all nations can join you in your kingdom. How are you going to spread the good news and gather them in?' Jesus responds by pointing to his small group of followers on earth. Gabriel says, 'Yes, Lord, but what other plans do you have?' Jesus says, 'I have no other plans.'

That may be an apocryphal story, but it speaks a truth. In the mystery of his sovereignty, God has chosen fallible, sinful human beings, like you and me, to further his mission on earth. It is a huge privilege, but also a great responsibility. The task is way beyond us, but it comes with a wonderful reassurance.

'Always'

Jesus said, 'I am with you always, to the very end of the age' (Matthew 28:18). We are not left to engage in mission on our own; Jesus is with us.

7. The proclaimed kingdom – the gospel goes to the ends of the earth

The book of Acts

The book of Acts begins with the disciples and the risen Jesus in Jerusalem. There is great expectation and they ask him, 'Lord, are you at this time going to restore the kingdom to Israel?' (Acts 1:6). It seems they still have a mainly nationalistic concept of salvation. Jesus replies, 'It is not for you to know the times or dates the Father has set by his own authority. But you will receive power when the Holy Spirit comes on you; and you will be my witnesses in Jerusalem, and in all Judea and Samaria, and to the ends of the earth' (Acts 1:7–8). The end will come only after the Spirit has thrust them out as Jesus' witnesses to all nations.

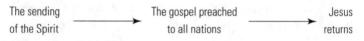

Figure 27. A chronology of the last days

Pentecost

This was an exclusively Jewish event; no Gentiles were present. But there are clear signs in Luke's account in Acts 2 that the coming of the Spirit will have global implications. Jews from 'every nation under heaven' (v. 2) are present as they hear the Spirit-filled disciples speaking in their own languages. It is a sign that Babel is about to be reversed. God scattered the nations there, but now he will gather them. The salvation Jesus offers will not be limited to the Jews. Peter tells the crowd, 'The promise is for you and your children and for all who are far off – for all whom the Lord our God will call' (2:39). From this start in Jerusalem, the gospel will go out to the ends of the earth as Isaiah had predicted, 'The law will go out from Zion, the word of the LORD from Jerusalem' (Isaiah 2:3).

The rest of Acts describes the message of Christ gradually going out to all nations. There are a few key moments in that process.

The conversion of Paul

The risen Jesus tells Saul on the Damascus Road to go to Ananias to have his sight restored. Ananias is understandably nervous about meeting this notorious persecutor of Christians, but the

Lord reassures him, 'This man is my chosen instrument to carry my name before the Gentiles and their kings and before the people of Israel' (Acts 9:15). He will be the apostle to the nations ('Gentiles' means 'nations').[4]

The conversion of Cornelius

Peter is prepared for the visit of Cornelius, a Roman centurion, by a vision in which he is commanded to eat food that was forbidden in the Jewish law. When he resists, a voice tells him, 'Do not call anything impure that God has made clean' (10:15). It is a sign that those laws that had previously marked the Jews as separate from the Gentiles were soon to be removed. Peter understands the message and welcomes Cornelius when he arrives, saying, 'God has shown me that I should not call any man impure or unclean' (10:28). He then preaches the gospel, beginning, 'I now realise how true it is that God does not show favouritism, but accepts men from every nation who fear him and do what is right' (10:34–35). Cornelius and his companions believe the message and the Holy Spirit comes on them. Luke tells us that the Jewish believers with Peter 'were astonished that the gift of the Holy Spirit had been poured out even on the Gentiles' (10:45).

It is likely that the Ethiopian eunuch was the first Gentile convert (8:25–40), although it seems that news of his conversion did not reach Jerusalem quickly. But reports about Cornelius soon cause controversy there. However, when Peter explains what had happened, they rejoice that God had 'granted even the Gentiles repentance unto life' (11:18). The mission to the Gentiles has been accepted.

Paul in Rome

Acts ends with Paul in Rome, the centre of the known world. It is worth noting that he is there to appeal to the emperor, having been arrested in Jerusalem. Just as Jesus suffered, so his witnesses should expect to suffer in his service. It was Paul's practice to preach to the Jews first when he arrived somewhere, and he does the same in Rome. Some believe, but many reject his message as the prophets had predicted (28:25–27). Paul concludes, 'Therefore I want you to know that God's salvation has been sent to the Gentiles, and they will listen!' (28:28). The book ends on that note, with Paul preaching to the Gentiles. The pattern that we have observed in Jesus' life and teaching is continued. We now live in the period after Israel has rejected Jesus, when the kingdom of God is offered to all nations.

John Stott has pointed to five pairs that feature consistently in the gospel proclamation of the apostles.[5]

- *Two gospel events*: Christ's death and resurrection (Acts 2:23–24; 1 Corinthians 15:3–5). The Christian message is not simply an idea. It is rooted in history. It is all about Jesus, who really lived, died and rose again.
- *Two gospel witnesses*: The Old Testament Scriptures (Acts 26:22–23; 1 Corinthians 15:3–4) and the witness of the apostles (Acts 2:32; 3:15). The apostles referred to the Old Testament Scriptures and their own eyewitness testimony to substantiate their claims about Jesus.
- *Two gospel affirmations*: Jesus is Lord and Saviour (Acts 2:36; 5:31). Jesus has ascended into heaven and has authority as Lord to demand submission, and as Saviour to give salvation. 'Salvation is found in no-one else, for there is no other name under heaven given to men by which we must be saved' (Acts 4:12).
- *Two gospel promises*: forgiveness of sins and the gift of the Spirit (Acts 2:38). These two great gifts are received simultaneously by those who turn to Christ.
- *Two gospel demands*: repentance and faith (Acts 2:38; 16:31). The apostles called on people to respond to the message of Jesus with trust and obedience. Baptism expressed both God's grace towards converts and their response to him.

Figure 28. What is the gospel?

The epistles

The church of Christ

The epistles are missionary documents. They are mostly written by church-planters to newly established congregations and deal with issues of belief and behaviour that have arisen. The apostles teach some remarkable truths about the Christian church, using Old Testament terms that had previously had an exclusively Jewish reference. God's church, made up of Jewish and Gentile believers, are *children of Abraham*, *God's household* and *the new temple*.

First, Paul teaches that the true *children of Abraham* are not his racial descendants, but those, Jew and Gentile, who are justified by faith in Christ (Romans 1:28–29). He tells the Galatians, 'Understand, then, that those who believe are children of Abraham. The Scripture foresaw that God would justify the Gentiles by faith, and announced the gospel in advance to Abraham: "All nations will be blessed through you"' (Galatians 3:7–9).

Secondly, Gentiles were formerly 'separate from Christ, excluded from citizenship in Israel and foreigners to the covenants of promise, without hope and without God in the world' (Ephesians 2:12). But the death of Christ has opened a way back to God for all people. The old divisions between Jews and Gentiles have been broken down in Christ. 'His purpose was to create in himself one new man out of the two, thus making peace, and in this one body to reconcile both of them to God through the cross, by which he put to death their hostility' (Ephesians 2:15–16). Jews and Gentiles together have access back to God through Christ. As a result Gentiles are 'no longer foreigners and aliens, but fellow-citizens with God's people and *members of God's household*' (Ephesians 2:19, my emphasis). The great privileges that were previously limited to the Jews are now enjoyed by the church. Peter, writing to a mixed group of Jewish and Gentile Christians, tells them, 'But you are a chosen people, a royal priesthood, a holy nation, a people belonging to God, that you may declare the praises of him who called you out of darkness into his wonderful light' (1 Peter 2:9).

Thirdly, Isaiah had foretold:

> In the last days
> the mountain of the Lord's temple will be established
>   as chief among the mountains;
> it will be raised above the hills,
>   and all nations will stream to it.
> (2:4)

That promise was fulfilled in the church. They understood themselves to be the *new temple* of which the prophets spoke. The Lord Jesus is the foundation or cornerstone (Ephesians 2:20; 1 Peter 2:4, 6–7) and believers are the stones (1 Peter 2:5). Jesus spoke of himself as the temple (John 2:19–22). It is as believers come to him, not to Jerusalem, that they become part of God's new building.

'All Israel will be saved'

Paul is deeply distressed at the unbelief, and consequent exclusion from Christ, of most of his own people. In Romans 9 – 11 he considers the place of Israel in God's plan of salvation. We can discern three stages in his understanding of what is happening in the present and what will happen in the future. Stage one is the rejection of Christ by Israel (the theme of Romans 10). But that sad reality had a positive result, which is the second stage: the gospel went to the Gentiles.

The Gentiles had no reason to be proud that they had received God's message. Even if many Jews had been broken off from God's people, like branches from an olive tree, the fact remains that the root and the tree are Jewish. God's work of salvation is based on his promises to the patriarchs. Gentile believers have not replaced the original tree; they have been unnaturally grafted into it. If God can do that, then he can certainly restore the natural branches (Romans 11:17–24).

That future restoration is Paul's third stage. He hopes that the conversion of Gentiles will arouse some of his own people to envy and lead to their salvation (Romans 11:11, 13–14). There will be Jews turning to their Messiah throughout the last days, but Paul seems to expect a very large number to do so at the end of time. He writes, 'Israel has experienced a hardening in part until the full number of the Gentiles has come in. And so all Israel will be saved' (Romans 11:25–26). Christians have differed as to how these words should be understood. Paul seems to be saying that, once the total number of Gentiles has turned to Christ, many Jews will do so too. The number will be so great that they will represent the whole race. If we are left with questions about how this might happen, we should respond with Paul and praise our great God, whose thoughts are far beyond us; 'O, the depths of the riches of the wisdom and knowledge of God!' (Romans 11:33).

Israel rejects Jesus ⟶ Salvation comes to the Gentiles ⟶ All Israel will be saved

Figure 29. All Israel will be saved

8. The perfected kingdom – God's multi-national family

After this I looked and there before me was a great multitude that no-one could count, from every nation, tribe, people and language, standing before the throne and in front of the Lamb. They were wearing white robes and were holding palm branches in their hands. And they cried out in a loud voice:

'Salvation belongs to our God,
who sits on the throne,
and to the Lamb.'
(Revelation 7:9–10)

The fruit of God's work of mission will be fully seen only in heaven. Only there will his promise to Abraham to bless all nations be completely fulfilled. One great family gathered from all nations, tribes and peoples will be joined together in his presence and there will be no confusion in their praises. No-one will be praising Allah, Krishna or the Buddha. All will worship the one God who has saved them through the Lamb, the Lord Jesus Christ. They are together in the New Jerusalem, as Isaiah had prophesied (Isaiah 2:2–4). This place is infinitely greater than any city that has existed on earth: 'The city does not need the sun or the moon to shine on it, for the glory of God gives it light, and the Lamb is its lamp. The nations will walk by its light, and the kings of the earth will bring their splendour into it' (Revelation 21:23–24).

Conclusion

Our part in God's mission to the Gentiles

We should speak to God about people

'Devote yourselves to prayer, being watchful and thankful. And pray for us, too, that God may open a door for our message, so that we may proclaim the mystery of Christ, for which I am in chains. Pray that I may proclaim it clearly, as I should' (Colossians 4:2–4).

In the mystery of God's sovereignty, he chooses to call people to Christ through the proclamation of the gospel in answer to prayer. Our prayer really can make a difference. Paul knew that, which is why he asked the Colossians to be committed in prayer for him.

No Christian was officially allowed to live in Nepal before 1960. In 1959 there were only 29 known believers there. But Christians prayed and a door for gospel outreach slowly opened. By 1985 there were an estimated 50,000 believers, rising to 200,000 in 1990, at a time of severe persecution. By 2000 the figure was somewhere between 400,000 and 500,000.[6] That represents an astonishing answer to prayer. But the door to many other nations and people-groups remains closed, either because missionaries are forbidden to enter or the people's hearts are hard.

There are 205 people-groups in Yunnan province in China with no witness to Christ and no Christians. Who will pray?[7]

Christian evangelism is strictly forbidden in Saudi Arabia, one of the least-evangelized nations on earth. Its 20 million Muslims have little chance of hearing the good news of Christ. Who will pray?[8]

'Of the world's 12,000 ethno linguistic peoples, about 3,000–3,600 are "world A" peoples in which less than 50% are likely to have heard the gospel. Nearly all originate from the 10/40 Window area',[9] which includes North Africa, the Middle East and South and East Asia. Who will pray?

We should speak to people about Jesus
'Be wise in the way you act towards outsiders; make the most of every opportunity. Let your conversation be always full of grace, seasoned with salt, so that you may know how to answer everyone' (Colossians 4:5–6).

Mission begins wherever we are, as we look for, and make the most of, opportunities to talk about Christ to friends, neighbours and colleagues. All Christians are called to be missionaries. We should be committed to the task of evangelism throughout our country, in the estates and villages, among people of every racial group and all ages.

God is making the task of reaching the nations easier by bringing them to us. The Western world is increasingly multi-racial and multi-national. Recently, a British diplomat was taken around a Chinese museum and, when he thanked his guide for showing him the nation's treasures, the guide replied, 'Our greatest treasures are in your country.' He was referring to the many Chinese who are sent to the West to study. We have a wonderful opportunity to show them Christian love and share the gospel with them while they are here. There are many like them from other nations too.

If most of us will be involved in the work of mission in our home countries, there is still an urgent need for others to go into cross-cultural settings overseas.

France is one of the most secular countries on earth. There are 15,000 more occult practitioners than Christian workers.[10] Who will go?

There are only 2 million professing Christians in Japan out of a population of 127 million.[11] The constitution guarantees freedom of religion and missionaries are able to get visas. Who will go?

Over 160 ethnic groups and 40 language groups are without viable indigenous congregations in Pakistan.[12] Expatriate Christian workers are still free to enter the country. Who will go?

In other countries, such as those in Sub-Saharan Africa, the need is often not so much for evangelists as for Bible teachers to train the pastors. Who will go?

One day the Lord Jesus will return to gather his people from every nation, tribe and people on earth. Until then, we have a great task that remains unfinished. But we are not left to do it on our own. Christ has given us his Spirit and his promise still remains: 'surely I am with you always, to the very end of the age' (Matthew 28:20).

Summary

1. The pattern of the kingdom (*Genesis 1 – 2*)	The Creator of all peoples
2. The perished kingdom (*Genesis 3*)	The human race is divided from God and each other
3. The promised kingdom (*Genesis 12*)	God promises to bless the nations
4. The partial kingdom (*Exodus – 2 Chronicles*)	Some Gentiles are drawn to Israel's God
5. The prophesied kingdom (*Ezra – Malachi*)	The nations will see God's glory
6. The present kingdom (*Gospels*)	The kingdom of Jesus is for all nations
7. The proclaimed kingdom (*Acts – Revelation*)	The gospel goes to the ends of the earth
8. The perfected kingdom	God's multi-national family

Figure 30. God and the nations

☐ Bible study

Isaiah 66:18–24

What is the goal of mission?

What are the main features of Isaiah's vision?

How should we understand the following today:
- 'Brothers' (verse 20) – see John 11:51–52

- 'Jerusalem' (verse 20) – see Hebrews 12:22–24;
  Revelation 21:1–2

- 'Priests' (verse 21) – see 1 Peter 2:5–9

- The unquenched fire – see Mark 9:47–48

In what ways is this vision fulfilled:
• Now?

• At the end of time (see Revelation 7:9–12)?

What implications should there be for:
• Our prayer life?

• The way we relate to different races, at home and abroad?

• Our ambitions?

• Our use of money?

• Our church's priorities?

Conclusion

How will you respond the next time someone says, 'You can make the Bible say anything you like', or asks you what the Bible teaches about prayer, work or heaven? The Bible is not an encyclopaedia in which you can look up a subject and find all the teaching on it presented in one place. It is more like a history book, or even a biography of God, describing what he has done and will do in the world. To find his mind on any subject, we must not turn to just one or two selected verses; we should rather seek to discern the teaching of the whole Bible as it develops through the different stages of salvation history. I have tried to show how that might be done with six subjects. I hope that has given you a model that you can apply to other themes.

Perhaps the key point to remember in studying the Bible is that it is, above all, a book about Jesus Christ. You will not go far wrong if you keep your eyes fixed on him. He is the centre to which the Old Testament points and from which the New Testament proceeds. The great purpose of the Bible is that we may know God the Father through him and then live lives that honour him. Let us make sure that the truths we have studied in this book do not stay in our heads, but warm our hearts, stir our wills and change our actions, so that Christ's name is glorified.

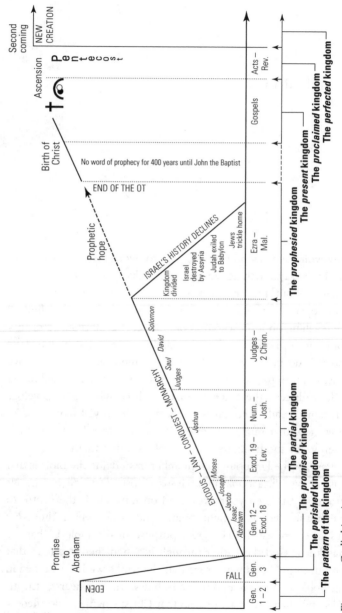

Figure 31. God's big picture

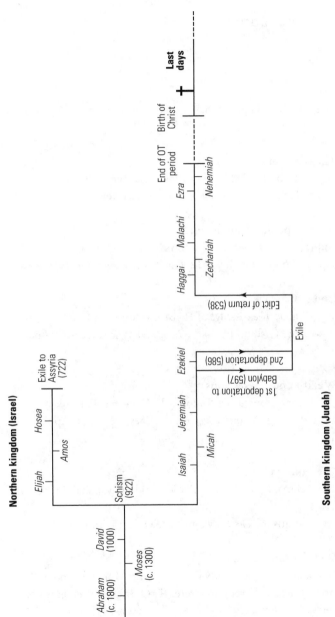

Northern kingdom (Israel)

Abraham (c. 1800)

Moses (c. 1300)

David (1000)

Schism (922)

Elijah   *Amos*   *Hosea*

Exile to Assyria (722)

Southern kingdom (Judah)

Isaiah   *Micah*   *Jeremiah*   *Ezekiel*

1st deportation to Babylon (597)

2nd deportation (586)

Exile

Edict of return (538)

Haggai   *Malachi*   *Zechariah*   *Ezra*   *Nehemiah*

End of OT period

Birth of Christ

Last days

Figure 32. A timeline of Bible history (not to scale)

Further reading

Under each heading, the first book is written at a simpler level than the second.

1. The once and future King
Vaughan Roberts, *God's Big Picture* (Leicester: IVP, 2003).
Donald Macleod, *The Person of Christ* (Leicester: IVP, 1998).

2. Naked ape or divine image?
David Jackman, *Humanity* (Milton Keynes: SU, 1986).
Philip Edgcumbe Hughes, *The True Image* (Leicester: IVP, 1989).

3. God's marriage
Derek Kidner, *The Message of Hosea* (Leicester: IVP, 1981).
Raymond C. Ortlund Jr, *God's Unfaithful Wife* (Leicester: Apollos, 1996).

4. Wealth and possessions
Brian Rosner, *How to Get Really Rich* (Leicester: IVP, 1999).
Craig Blomberg, *Neither Poverty nor Riches* (Leicester: Apollos, 1999).

5. The Holy Spirit
David Jackman, *The Spirit of Truth* (London: Marshall Pickering, 1993).
Sinclair Ferguson, *The Holy Spirit* (Leicester: IVP, 1996).

6. God and the nations
Robin Wells, *My Rights, My God* (London: Monarch, 2000).
Andreas J. Köstenberger and Peter T. O'Brien, *Salvation to the Ends of the Earth* (Leicester: Apollos, 2001).

Notes

Introduction

1 *Oxford Student*, 20 May 1999.

1. The once and future King

1 See Graeme Goldsworthy, *Gospel and Kingdom* (Exeter: Paternoster, 1981).

2 Ibid., p. 47.

3 See Galatians 3:8.

4 See Romans 16:20; Revelation 20:2.

5 Christ simply means 'anointed one'. The kings of Israel were anointed with oil.

6 See Acts 4:21.

7 Revelation 2:7, 11, 17, 26; 3:5, 12, 21.

2. Naked ape or divine image?

1 *The Human Body*, BBC, May 1998.

2 Quoted in John Blanchard, *Does God Believe in Atheists?* (Darlington: Evangelical Press, 2000), p. 317.

3 Quoted in ibid., pp. 334–335.

4 Richard Dawkins, *The Selfish Gene* (Oxford: Oxford University Press, 1989).

5 Desmond Morris, *The Naked Ape* (New York: Dell, 1967), p. 9.

6 Wayne Grudem, *Systematic Theology* (Leicester: IVP, 1994), pp. 446–447.

7 David Watson, *In Search of God* (London: Falcon, 1974), p. 39.

8 J. John, *What's the Point of Christmas?* (Oxford: Lion), p. 41.

9 John Henry Newman, 'Praise to the Holiest in the height', verse 2, in *Christian Praise* (London: Tyndale Press, 1957).

10 John Calvin, *Institutes of the Christian Religion* (ed. J. T. McNeill, trans. Ford Lewis Battles) (Philadelphia: Westminster, 1960), 3.1.53.

11 John Stott, *Focus on Christ* (London: Fount, 1979), pp. 53–54.

12 William Temple, *Citizen and Churchman* (London: Eyre & Spottiswoode, 1941), p. 2.

3. God's marriage

1 *The Times*, 10 June 2000.

2 Nick Pollard, *Why Do They Do That?* (Oxford: Lion, 1998), p. 47.

3 Quoted in John Blanchard, *Does God Believe in Atheists?* (Darlington: Evangelical Press, 2000), p. 519.

4 'Marriage' in *New Dictionary of Biblical Theology* (Leicester: IVP, 2000), p. 656.

5 Raymond Ortlund Jr, *Whoredom* (Leicester: Apollos, 1996), now entitled *God's Unfaithful Wife*, p. 156.

6 Ibid.

7 Christopher Ash, *Marriage* (Leicester: IVP, 2003).

8 Ibid.

9 'Marriage' in *New Dictionary of Biblical Theology*, p. 657.

10 'A life in the day of Grant Bovey', *The Sunday Times*, August 2000.

11 Jimmy Hill, quoted in John Blanchard, *Does God Believe in Atheists?*, p. 384.

12 Anne Morrow Lindbergh, *Hour of Gold, Hour of Lead* (Orlando: Harvest Books, 1993), Introduction.

4. Wealth and possessions

1 Nicky and Jackie Singer, *The Little Book of the Millennium* (Sevenoaks: Hodder Headline, 1999).

2 *The Sunday Times*, 19 November 2000.

3 R. Kent Hughes, *The Supremacy of Christ* (Leicester: Crossway, 1989), p. 90.

4 *Church Times*, 1 September 2000.

5 Ronald J. Sider, *Rich Christians in an Age of Hunger*
(Sevenoaks: Hodder, 1990), p. 122.

5. The Holy Spirit

1 Sinclair Ferguson, *The Holy Spirit* (Leicester: IVP, 1996), p. 17.
2 Michael Green, *I Believe in the Holy Spirit* (London: Hodder,
1975), p. 20.
3 J. I. Packer, *Keep in Step with the Spirit* (Leicester: IVP, 1984),
p. 65.
4 Ibid., p. 66.
5 John Stott, *Baptism and Fullness* (Leicester: IVP, 1975), p. 36.
6 David Wells, *God the Evangelist* (Grand Rapids: Eerdmans,
1987), p. 34.
7 See chapter 6, 'God and the nations'.

6. God and the nations

1 David Watson, *Fear No Evil* (London: Hodder, 1984), p. 128.
2 Graeme Goldsworthy, quoted in Andreas Köstenberger and
Peter T. O'Brien, *Salvation to the Ends of the Earth* (Leicester:
Apollos, 2001), p. 35.
3 John Piper, *Let the Nations be Glad* (Leicester: IVP, 1986), p. 11.
4 Romans 1:5; 15:16; Galatians 1:16–17.
5 John Stott, *Christian Mission in the Modern World*
(Eastbourne: Kingsway, 1986), pp. 44–54.
6 Patrick Johnstone and Jason Mandryk, *Operation World* (21st
Century Edition; Carlisle: Paternoster, 2001), p. 470.
7 Ibid., p. 180.
8 Ibid., pp. 556–557.
9 Ibid., p. 15.
10 Ibid., p. 256.
11 Ibid., p. 370.
12 Ibid., p. 502.